THE ORIGINAL

Birdhouse Book

Building Houses, Feeders, and Baths

By DON McNEIL

BirdWatcher's DIGEST®

Bird Watcher's Digest Press,
P. O. Box 110, Marietta, Ohio 45750
(740) 373-5285 or 800-879-2473   www.birdwatchersdigest.com
1979 by Don McNeil.
©2012 Bird Watcher's Digest Press

Printed in the United States of America.
Second printing 1981, Third printing 1982, Fourth printing 1983
Fifth printing 1985, Sixth printing 1987, Seventh printing 1991
Printings 8–16, 1993–2008, Revised and updated 2002
Edited by Bill Thompson, III, and Deborah Griffith
Schematic drawings by Don McNeil
Bird illustrations by Julie Zickefoose
Cover design by Claire Mullen
Production by Andrew T. Stout, Bill Thompson, III

Front cover images (*from top left, clockwise*):
Male tree swallow by Marie Read
Bird house maintenance by Bill Thompson, III
Eastern bluebird eggs by Bill Thompson, III
Female eastern bluebird by Maslowski Photography
Winter bluebird house by Julie Zickefoose
Carolina wren by Maslowski Photography
Eastern bluebird female by Bill Thompson, III
Eastern bluebird hatchlings by Bill Thompson, III
Carolina chickadee nestlings by Maslowski Photography
Male eastern bluebird by Maslowski Photography

Library of Congress Cataloging in Publication Data
McNeil, Don.
    The birdhouse book.

    Bibliography: p.
    1. Bird-houses—Design and construction. 2. Bird feeders—
Design and construction. 3. Birdbaths—Design and construction. I. Title.
QL676.5.M332   690'.8'9   79-254
ISBN 0-914718-36-3

Foreword

In 1924 at age four, Don McNeil came west with his parents from Kansas to settle in Raymond, Washington. He grew up in Olympia and at nine years old built his first birdhouse to attract violet-green swallows. House sparrows evicted them, and McNeil has disliked these sparrows ever since.

After McNeil finished high school the family moved to Salem, Oregon. He spent a year at Park College in Missouri, then entered the University of Oregon, where he majored in English and drama. He finished college after serving 22 months in the Army Air Corps in China and India during World War II.

From 1948 until 1972 he managed chambers of commerce in Lakeview, Seaside, Medford, and Salem, Oregon, and there was always a birdhouse in his backyard.

McNeil's freelance writing began in the mid-1970s and his *Birdhouse Book* was first published by Pacific Search Press in 1979. Now retired, McNeil continues to write. In an effort to bring back some of the tree swallows whose numbers seem to have diminished, he currently maintains 25 birdhouses at the Neskowin golf course on the Oregon Coast.

Dedication

To my wife, Anna, whose faith in me is beyond belief

Special Thanks

I am especially indebted to the following people, whose knowledge and generous sharing of information have helped greatly in preparing this book: Hubert Prescott and Al Prigge for their outstanding accomplishments with western bluebirds; Tom Lund for his invaluable information about purple martin colonies in Oregon; Charles Bruce of the Oregon Fish and Wildlife Department for his advice on wood ducks; and James Parsons and James L. Payne for their practical suggestions about wood duck boxes.

Introduction to the Revised Edition

Don McNeil's *Original Birdhouse Book* is a classic in the pantheon of reference and how-to books for the backyard bird watcher. It has been a best-seller since its first printing in 1979. In the years since then we have learned a great deal about backyard birds and what we offer to them in the form of feeders, houses, and foods has changed. In 1979 there was no such thing as a suet cake. Tube and hopper feeders were the rule, but black oil sunflower seed was just becoming available for bird feeding.

Today a bird watcher can shop almost anywhere for excellent products for backyard birds and nature.

In 2002, *Bird Watcher's Digest* Press initiated a full updated revision of *The Original Birdhouse Book*. We hope this new, improved version will help to enhance your enjoyment of the birds and nature in your own backyard.—Bill Thompson, III, Editor, *Bird Watcher's Digest*

Please Note

The original intent of this book was to provide complete, simple instructions for building bird houses, feeders, baths, and other devices for the backyard using simple and inexpensive materials. A few concepts and ideas from the earlier editions of this book will benefit from some clarification.

Wood for Building

While Don McNeil originally suggested using exterior plywood or scrap pieces of T-111 siding for bird house and feeder construction, we suggest western red cedar as a longer-lasting alternative. Many commercial feeder manufacturers today rely totally on cedar for durable, lightweight, weather-resistant bird house construction. If your region has significant periods of wet, rainy weather, cedar may be a better alternative than plywood or siding pieces. If your region is arid or mostly dry during the birds' nesting season, almost any type of wood can be used, provided it is treated on the outside with a weather sealant.

Nails versus Screws

When constructing your houses and feeders based on the instructions in this book, consider using wood screws rather than nails for sturdier construction.

Placement, Mounting, and Baffles

Before nailing your newly built bird house to a nearby tree or fence post, learn which nest-box predators are present in your area. If you have raccoons, squirrels, snakes, weasels, oppossums, or feral or neighborhood cats, consider mounting your birdhouse on a predator-proof pole. In areas with concentrated predator populations unbaffled nest boxes or boxes mounted on trees and fence posts will only serve to benefit the predators, and not the nesting birds. See "Predators and Competitors" on page 72 for some easy-to-make baffle designs.—*Bill Thompson, III, editor, 2002 revised edition*

Contents

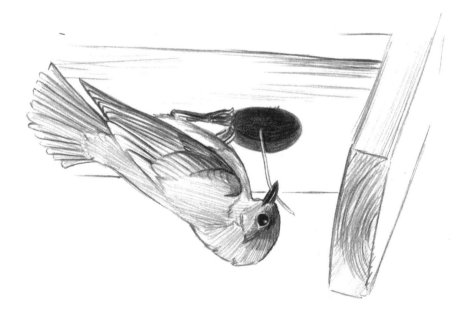

mean that you will attract wrens, unless they are naturally found in your area. Start by getting a good bird book that is designed for your locality. Your local book stores, library, or the local bird club, Nature Conservancy, or Audubon Society chapter can help you. The purpose of this information is to give you a general idea about the birds you may attract. Next put a bird feeder in your yard and observe the birds that visit it regularly. Among the avian visitors to your yard will be a few species that will nest in your birdhouses (cavity-nesting birds) and a few that may take advantage of a nesting or roosting shelf. More than a few species will be interested in your bird feeders. And all birds can appreciate a good source of water.

The first house described in this book is easily built and will attract various kinds of birds. Even if you are an experienced woodworker or want to build another house first, read the introductory material in "A Simple Birdhouse." It explains how to use the instructions and drawings for all the other plans.

A bluebird checks a nest box interior.

Getting Started

Attracting birds offers excitement and challenges, not only because there is so much even experts do not know, but also because birds are always coming up with new tricks to defeat our most carefully contrived plans. You will glow with satisfaction, then, when a bird nests, feeds, or bathes in something you have built. If it is a species you have been trying to attract, you will begin to think of yourself as a specialist. And, in a sense, you are.

This book is not strictly for bird watchers. Instead, this is a simple book for the person who wants to build birdhouses (sometimes called nest boxes), feeders, and baths for a few birds, study how effective the plans are, and perhaps try a few innovations. Call us "bird culturalists," if you will—we encourage native birds by creating a favorable environment in miniature.

If you decide that you would like to provide bed and board for birds, first become familiar with a few general principles. Above all, take it easy! Do not rush out, buy lumber, and build every birdhouse shown in this book. Having a wren house, for example, does not

Birdhouse Basics

Whether you buy your nest boxes or build them from these plans, there are certain characteristics your housing should have to best suit the needs of nesting birds. Here are some nest box basics:

• The lumber used should be untreated and at least ¾-inch thick to protect nests from spring chills and summer heat. Exterior plywood, cedar, and pine work well.

• Do not paint or stain the inside of the box. If you paint or stain the outside of the box, use a light earth tone color latex so sunlight and heat will be reflected, not absorbed.

• Use galvanized screws to assemble the nest box. It will last years longer than one built with nails or with glue, which will not last as the wood warps and shrinks.

• Your access to the inside of the nest box should be easy for nest inspections and box maintenance. The best box designs feature a side or front panel that can be swung up or out to gain access to the inside.

• Perches on the front of a nest box are not necessary. All cavity nesters have strong feet and can easily cling to vertical wooden surfaces. Perches only give easy access to house sparrows, starlings, and predators.

• The roof of the nest box should extend well over the entrance hole to protect the opening from driving rain and predators.

• The inside front panel of the box should be deeply scored

below the hole to give emerging birds a ladder for exiting the box.

• The floor of the nest box should have at least four ⅜-inch drain holes so the box can drain if it does get wet. The floor should be recessed so that no end grain is exposed to soak up rain water.

• Ventilation holes near the top allow excess heat to escape. Plug holes with weather-stripping putty in cold weather.

• The nest box should be protected from predators. The best way to protect your nest boxes is to mount them on poles with a predator baffle in place below the box. (See the baffle design in the "Predators and Competitors" chapter starting on page 72.)

Housing Placement

Once you have housing, you need to place it in the right habitat. Use the information in this book to learn more about the birds you hope to attract.

Having selected a spot within appropriate habitat, make certain your nest boxes are securely mounted and baffled against predators (more about this topic later).

Monitoring and Record Keeping

You slowly open a nest box and see a black-capped chickadee sitting on its nest. What do you do? Simply close the box, walk away, and record in your notebook that the female was on the nest, probably incubating eggs. This scenario underscores the reason nest boxes should be easy to open from the front or side. Spending several minutes disassembling a nest box to check its contents can be enough to drive a nesting bird away permanently.

If the female leaves as you approach, or as you open the box, inspect the nest quickly, record your findings, and leave the area. Your complete visit should take no more than 30 seconds. If you are able to keep your visit this brief, the female will return to the nest box shortly.

If you know the species using your nest box, learn about its incubation period—usually about two weeks from the laying of the last egg to the hatching date. If you know the approximate date egg-laying ended and incubation began, you can estimate the hatching date of the eggs. This is important information. Timing is everything for a nest-box landlord. If you visit the nest during incubation or late in the nestling stage, you may cause nest abandonment or premature fledging. A good general rule is to limit nest box visits to the 10 days immediately after hatching. Resist the urge to visit nestlings—appealing as they may be—more often than necessary.

Observing and recording the progress of active nests is perhaps the most fascinating aspect of being a landlord to cavity nesting birds. For most of the nesting season, a weekly visit to each box will provide an accurate snapshot of the lives of your birds, without undue disturbance.

Devote a separate field notebook to your nest boxes, allowing several pages per nest. Record what you see during your inspections. Include the following information: Is the box being used? By what species? Has courtship or nest building begun? If there is a nest in the box, what is it made of? If there are eggs, how many and what do they look like? Also record, hatching date, fledging date, and anything else you observe. Over time your records will help you to become a better landlord.

Keep in mind that all this activity requires patience because you will face many frustrations and setbacks. You will also have triumphs and, maybe best of all, another spring of excitement and challenges to which you may look forward. Are you ready? Then go to it!

A Simple Birdhouse

Once you figure out which birds feed in your area and which ones are cavity nesters, you can start building a simple birdhouse—one that is easy to put together and one that will attract a number of species. The instructions for this first house are designed for the novice, but if you are an experienced "builder," you also will want to be familiar with the introductory information because it explains how to use the drawings and instructions in this book. Having learned the general building principles here, you can go on to more challenging projects, which will not have every step spelled out, but which will also attract more unusual nesters.

With any of the birdhouse plans and instructions in this book, *read and study everything before starting to build the birdhouse.* This will make the building go more smoothly and should prevent costly, frustrating errors. Study the instructions and drawings together. The letters in the instructions refer to the drawing that illustrates a particular section of directions.

Now, let's look at materials. Cedar will last, but it can be expensive. Pound for pound, cedar is the most durable, weather resistant, and provides the best insulation. After years of weather, nails in cedar can become loose, so I suggest using screws in place of nails for cedar construction. Pine is easy to nail and does not split easily, but it will decay unless preservatives are used. Birds are better off without the latter. An excellent alternative material is ⅝-inch thick exterior plywood, which I have suggested for almost all the houses described in this book. It is tough, weathers well, and will not split along the edge if you use nails of the proper size, usually fourpenny galvanized box nails. Called T 1-11, this wood has vertical grooves to resemble boards and is often used for siding on homes. Scraps at construction sites are frequently either burned or hauled away (what a waste!), so ask the carpenters for a few pieces. They can probably fix you up.

When assembling a house using exterior plywood, always remember to keep the weather surface of the wood on the outside of the birdhouse. It is an obvious point, but one that is easily forgotten in the midst of the building process. Unless otherwise instructed, use fourpenny galvanized box nails for nailing house parts together. Remember to use screws when using cedar or pine, or when you feel extra strong binding is necessary.

It will be a household guessing game as to which species is most apt to settle in your new birdhouse. Half a dozen cavity-nesting birds like a box with a single slant roof and a 1½-inch-diameter entrance. Depending on your location, it could be tree swallows, violet-green swallows, hairy woodpeckers, perhaps titmice, chickadees, or even bluebirds.

In all likelihood it will be English sparrows, also known as house sparrows, which are not sparrows at all, but belong to the weaver finch family of Africa. House sparrows were brought from England to New York City in the 1850s and spread to the West Coast by the 1890s. These little strutters now live in almost everybody's neighborhood, seeming to thrive wherever humans live. Easily identified, the males are brown on the back with light wing bars, and gray underneath with a black throat patch, gray cheeks, and gray on the top of the head. While they chirp incessantly, singing is quite out of the question. The females are quite plain, but industrious and aggressive.

Being early nesters, house sparrows generally occupy birdhouses before bluebirds or swallows do. The male house sparrow selects the nesting site, entering several times in order to coax the female inside. He will even start nest building activities, bringing bits of straw, feathers, or whatever is readily available. He is an aggressive

Chickadees are cavity nesters that readily take to nest boxes.

defender of his territory, tolerating no other birds nesting nearby. House sparrows are seed eaters, although their diet in summer is predominantly insects, which they feed to their young--usually five or six scrawny creatures with voracious appetites. Two and sometimes three broods are raised each year. See "Predators and Competitors" for more information on dealing with nest box competitors.

Materials

Western red cedar, or exterior plywood, ⅝ in., 31 by 14 in.; or T 1-11 siding scraps:

- Bottom—5 by 5 in.
- Sides (2)—each 10 by 6¼ in.
- Back—12 by 6¼ in.
- Front—9½ by 6¼ in.
- Roof—8¾ by 8¼ in.
- Fourpenny galvanized box nails
- Right-angle screw hook, about 1½ in. Long
- Caulking compound
- Sixteen-penny galvanized framing nail
- Galvanized siding nails (2),1¾ in. Long
- Post (optional)—2 in. by 4 in. by 8 ft. (Or see the baffle design on page 77 for a better alternative.)
- Prepared sand-mix concrete (optional), 1 sack
- Stakes (optional, 2)
- Boards (optional, 2), about 5 ft. Long

Tools

- Square
- Ruler
- Pencil
- Saw
- Plane
- Brace, with 1½-in. expansion bit and ½-in.-diameter bit
- C clamps (optional, 2)
- Rasp
- Hammer
- Wood blocks of various sizes
- Drill, with assorted small bits
- String (optional), 4 ft.
- Weight (optional)
- Large rocks (optional)

A Simple Birdhouse

A.

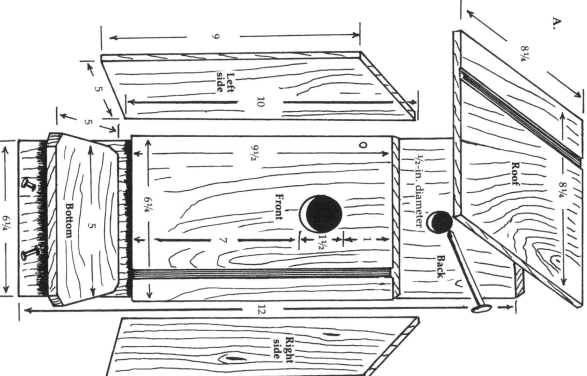

Note: Dimensions are in inches

Instructions

A. 1. On the weather surface of the plywood, measure and mark with a pencil the exact outlines of each piece. Be sure the grain of the wood runs vertically on the 2 side pieces, the back, and the front. The T 1-11 siding has a vertical groove running down it. This won't hurt anything. But when laying out the parts, keep the groove away from the edge of each piece so you later will not have problems with nailing.

2. Lay out the 2 side pieces with a common line along the 9-in. dimension so that the tops angle toward the center line, making a shallow V. In this way, when you assemble the house, the weather surface will end up on the outside.

3. After checking the measurements once more, carefully saw or cut out all the parts. Trim the rough edges with a plane to knock off splinters. (It saves Band-Aids.) You won't need to sand anything—this is going to be rustic!

4. Lay the parts on the workbench and mark them, just to keep track. There are 6—2 sides, a roof, bottom, front, and back.

5. To accommodate the roof slant, you will need to bevel the top edges of the front and back panels with a plane. Set the 2 pieces in front of you, just as they will be when assembled. On pieces in front of you, just as they will be when assembled. On the weather surface of the front panel and on the inside surface of the back, draw a horizontal line ⅛ in. down from the top. Then bevel off ⅛ in. from each piece individually.

6. On the front panel, center a vertical line running 3 in. down from the top. Put a cross mark on the line, 1¾ in. from the top. Open the expansion bit to precisely 1½ in., then test it on a scrap board and measure the hole. Now, to ensure a clean cut, clamp the panel tightly to a board. Center the bit on the cross mark and drill the hole. (If you have no C clamps, lay the panel on a board and drill halfway. Turn it over and drill through the other side.) Round off the sharp edges with a rasp.

7. On the bottom piece, measure ⅜ in. in on each side of each corner and mark. Place a ruler diagonally across each corner and connect the 2 marks. Saw off the 4 corners at these points.

The resultant openings in the finished house will allow adequate drainage and air circulation for the birds.

8. On the back panel, weather side up, center a vertical line, 2 in. down from the top. At the bottom of the line, drill a ½-in. long, down from the top. At the bottom of the line, drill a ½-in. hole.

9. Mark a line across the weather surface of both side panels, 1 in. up from the bottom. On the right panel, extend the bottom line across the edges. Mark a line across the face of the front panel, 1 in. up from the bottom. It, too, should extend across the edges.

10. Now, mark a line across the weather surface on the back panel, 2½ in. up from the bottom, and extend it across the edges.

B. 1. You are now ready to start putting things together. Lay the right-hand side panel (the one on the right when the entrance of the completed birdhouse faces you), weather surface up, on the bench. Start 2 nails, each 1½ in. in from the edge and ¼ in. below the bottom line. Drive them in until they barely peek through the other side. Be sure they are straight.

B.

2. Place the bottom panel (weather side toward you) on edge and at a right angle to the bench, against a flat wall or solid surface. (When the corners are cut off, it is easier to get the side and bottom flush when both are pressed against a flat wall.) Lay the right side panel (weather side out) across the upper edge of the bottom piece, matching the line on the side panel with the interior surface of the bottom. (Place a block under the other end of the right panel.) Drive the nails part way in, enough to hold.

C. 1. Turn the assembled pieces over so the right side faces you. Place 2 nails in the weather surface of the back panel, ¼ in. below the line you marked earlier and 1½ in. from the ends of the bottom panel. Drive them in until they begin to show on the other side.

2. Put the back piece on the 2 pieces that you assembled. Make sure that the lines marked on the bottom match and that the edges are flush with the outside of the side panel.

3. Drive the nail into the bottom, nearest the side panel, enough to hold. Start another nail along the edge of the back panel, 2 in. down from the top and about ¼ in. from the edge. Check to see that the back panel edge and the side are flush. Drive the nail part way in.

4. Now check the bottom. Its outer corner may be sprung slightly. Press it into alignment with the back panel marks, hold, and drive the other bottom nail part way in. Check it over to see if the bottom is lined up. If so, place one more nail along the edge, 4 in. up from the bottom of the back panel, and drive in all the nails.

D. 1. Turn the unit on its back. Lay out the front panel, weather side up—racing stripe dazzling your eyes—and start 2 nails ¼ in. below the bottom line and 1½ in. in from each edge. Be sure the points have just come through the other side.

2. Put the front in place, matching the lines marked at the bottom with the interior surface of the bottom panel. There should be about a ½-in. gap at the top of the right side when the roof is on.

3. Drive the nail into the bottom, nearest the enclosed side, until the nail holds. Then start a nail 2 in. down from the top of the

C.

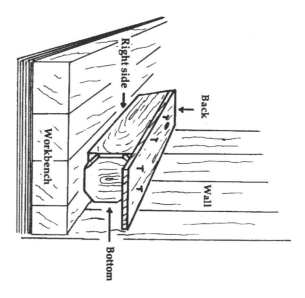

D.

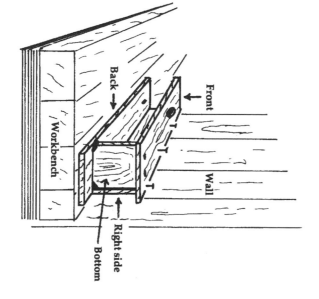

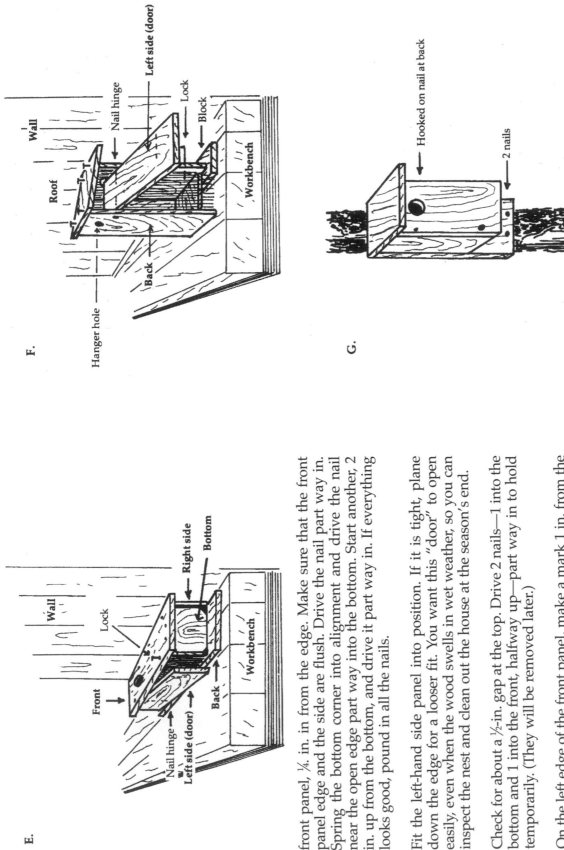

F.

Wall

Roof

Nail hinge

Left side (door)

Lock

Block

Workbench

Back

Hanger hole

G.

Hooked on nail at back

2 nails

The Original Birdhouse Book

E.

Wall

Lock

Right side

Bottom

Front

Nail hinge

Left side (door)

Back

Workbench

front panel, ¼ in. in from the edge. Make sure that the front panel edge and the side are flush. Drive the nail part way in. Spring the bottom corner into alignment and drive the nail near the open edge part way into the bottom. Start another, 2 in. up from the bottom, and drive it part way in. If everything looks good, pound in all the nails.

E. 1. Fit the left-hand side panel into position. If it is tight, plane down the edge for a looser fit. You want this "door" to open easily, even when the wood swells in wet weather, so you can inspect the nest and clean out the house at the season's end.

2. Check for about a ½-in. gap at the top. Drive 2 nails—1 into the bottom and 1 into the front, halfway up—part way in to hold temporarily. (They will be removed later.)

3. On the left edge of the front panel, make a mark 1 in. from the top. Using a square, draw a horizontal line across the left side panel on the mark. At one end of this line, drive a nail through the front panel into the edge of the left panel. At the other end of the line, drive a nail through the back panel into the edge of the left panel. These nail hinges will allow the "door" to be opened.

4. Put a mark on the front panel 2 in. up from the bottom and centered over the edge of the door. Drill a small hole, about 2 in. deep, at the mark. Use a right-angle screw hook, twisted into place, as a lock nail. It is not likely to fall out of the hole, as a nail might, when the box is tipped forward. Remove the temporary nails and test the door.

F. 1. On the roof, start 2 nails, each ¼ in. in from the back or top edge of the roof, and about 2 in. in from the left and right sides. Remember that the roof slants, and you want the nail angled so it goes straight into the edge of the back panel. Stand the box upright with a block under the front. Run a strip of caulking compound along the top edge of the back panel. Place the top on, with the wood grain running down the slant, not across it.

2. Adjust the roof for equal overhang on each side. It should be flush with the back. Drive the nail part way in.

3. Sight along the front and drive 2 more nails—gingerly—into the top edge of the front panel until they hold. If it looks right, hammer them in.

G. 1. Now for hanging the birdhouse. If you read the cautions about predators and birdhouses in this book's introduction and you've discovered that there are predators in your area, resist the temptation to hang your housing on a tree or fencepost. If your area is predator-free (and not many areas are in North America) trees may be OK. See "Predators and Competitors" beginning on page 72.

2. If you are mounting your house on a baffled 4x4 post, hammer in a sixteen-penny, galvanized framing nail at a slightly downward angle. Leave 1 in. sticking out. Hook the nail through the hole in the back of the house. Drive 2 galvanized siding nails into the trunk through the bottom of the back panel. It won't hurt to leave these protruding ¼ in. With a hammer you can easily pull the nails, unhook the birdhouse, and change locations.

H. 1. You also can mount this birdhouse on a 2-in. by 4-in. post, 8 ft. high. Dig a hole, then set the post in it. Drive 2 stakes, each 4 ft. from the post. Temporarily nail a board to each stake. These

should be long enough to reach 4 ft. up the post at an angle, and they should extend at right angles to each other. Set the post perpendicularly, using a 4-ft. length of string and a weight to check vertical alignment. Make adjustments and set the nails in the post to hold, but do not drive them in all the way. Drop some large rocks to fill space in the hole. Wet them down. Mix and pour prepared sand-mix concrete (setting the post in concrete allows the wood to last longer), using a stick to jiggle it down around the rocks. Let it cure for 1 week before mounting the birdhouse (see Step G 2).

2. If you hang your birdhouse on a tree trunk or post, then you'll need to put a predator guard below the house (see "Predators and Competitors" chapter on page 72).

3. You also can hang your birdhouse on the side of your own house, choosing a place that is inaccessible to predators.

H.

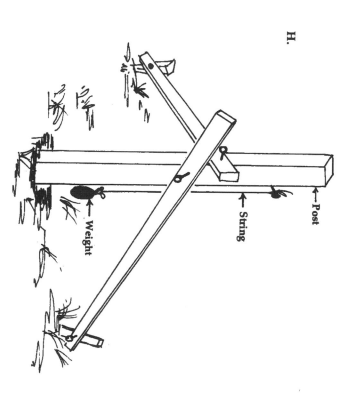

Post

String

Weight

Swallow Nest Boxes

According to estimates by one ornithologist, the average swallow daily consumes about 6,000 insects (mostly gnats and midges) in Orange County, California. About 10,000 swallows stay approximately 219 days a year in the area and eliminate some 13.4 billion insects each season.

That's one good reason for putting up birdhouses to attract swallows. They are also colorful birds whose acrobatic capabilities will add a dash of excitement around your home. Besides all this, certain species need help. The **violet-green swallows** are dwindling in number in western cities, perhaps because of the competition of non-native hole nesters. The **tree swallow** population also seems to be declining in areas where it has lost its wetland habitat. You can help these birds by providing nesting sites. But remember that one swallow does not make a summer. You, and all of us, will need to attract many more than that if we are to save some species.

The tree swallow and the violet-green swallow are cavity nesters and the most easily attracted of the swallow family. (A third spe-

*Violet-green swallows
are familiar users of
nest boxes in the West.*

cies, the purple martin, is described in the next chapter.) These two birds are often confused, but identification actually is quite simple. Both have white underparts, but the violet-green swallow also has white rump patches, easily spotted in flight. Its call is a high-pitched twittering. The tree swallow is slightly larger than the violet-green, its back is steely blue, and its call is a kind of low chortle. During summer nesting, it is found throughout the United States and southern Canada near water or wet meadows. It seldom penetrates cities unless proper habitat is available. The violet-green swallow, on the other hand, searches out nesting sites deep within cities west of the Rockies.

Both species arrive about the same time in early spring, from late February to mid-March, depending on the latitude. The male and female of both species share in the nest building activities, as they do in feeding the young, usually four to six little creatures with monumental appetites.

If either the tree swallow or the violet-green swallow frequents your neighborhood each spring, the two easily built houses described in this chapter will attract them.

Quick-Release Swallow Box

This house will give you lots of flexibility. It has a quick-release device so you can mount it on a baffled wooden post or under the eaves of your home in a matter of seconds. You can easily build several and give your swallows a choice of houses. You can also lure both species to nest in proximity as long as they cannot see each other from the entrance of their houses. Swallows squabble.

Materials

Cedar or exterior plywood, ⅝ in., 25¼ by 24¼ in.; or T 1-11 siding scraps:

    Bottom—10³h by 7 in.
    Sides (2)—each 7 by 7 in.
    Back—12 by 7 in.
    Front—12 by 7 in.
    Roof—14 by 10 in.

Fourpenny galvanized box nails
Galvanized nail or right-angle screw hook, about 1½ in. long
Angle strip—¾-in. straight-grained wood, about 12 in. long
Hardware cloth, ⅛-in. mesh, 12 by 8¼ in.

Staples, #5, wire brad

Post (optional)—2 in. by 4 in. by 10 ft.

Prepared sand-mix concrete (optional),

1 sack roofing nails (2),1½ in. long with ³⁄₈-in. head

Tools

Square	Pencil
Ruler	Saw
Rasp	Drill, with assorted small bits
Keyhole saw	Hammer
Plane	
Brace, with ½-in.-diameter bit and 1½-in. expansion bit	

Instructions

A. 1. Using a square, lay out all parts according to the dimensions shown, remembering that the weather surface of the wood should face out when the house is completed. Cut out all pieces.

2. On the bottom piece, make a mark ⅝ in. in on each side of each corner, then cut off the corners at these marks. (Air circulation is vital under the eaves.)

3. On the front piece, draw a vertical line 2½ in. from the right side and a horizontal line 2½ in. from the bottom. Clamp a scrap board behind the front panel (to allow a clean cut, then use a 1½-in. expansion bit to drill where the 2 lines you have drawn intersect. Rough the edges with a rasp.

4. To make the lock slots in the back panel, center a vertical line down the back piece. Drill a ½-in. hole on the line, 1 in. up from the bottom. Drill another ½-in. hole on the line, 1¼. in. down from the top.

5. With the keyhole saw, make two ½-in.-long cuts right next to each other up the center line from each of the 2 sides. Cut out the wood between both pairs of cuts. Test to see if the shaft of the roofing nail slips easily up and down the double cuts. File or sandpaper these cuts until smooth.

B. 1. Start the assembly by nailing the right side to the bottom, allowing ¼. in. of the side piece to hang below the bottom

Note: Dimensions are in inches

A.

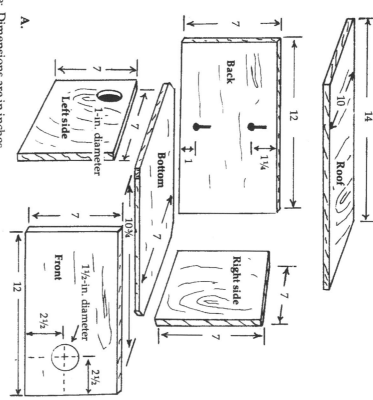

B.

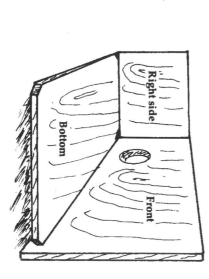

panel. Nail on the front panel so that the entrance is in the lower right corner and the front piece extends ¼ in. below the bottom piece.

At this point you need to decide if you want to install a removable trigger mechanism for trapping house sparrows. If so, turn to the chapter about predators and follow the instructions for either of the sparrow traps. It is easier to install the mechanism now rather than after the house is completed.

C. 1. To continue with the assembly, nail the back on, matching the bottom edge to give that ¼ in. drop.

2. The left side piece will be the door. Drill a 1-in. hole near the upper left corner. This allows additional air circulation and escapement for chickadees, should you ever use the house as a trap for house sparrows.

3. Fit the door in place. If it does not move easily in and out, then plane the edges. Draw a horizontal line ½ in. down from the top. Put the door in place and, aligning a nail and this line, drive the nail part way into the front piece and into the edge of the door. Repeat on the other side of the door, going through the back piece. Be sure the door swings easily. Then drive in all the nails.

4. Drill a small hole through the front piece and into the bottom edge of the door. Into this hole, push a 1½-in. galvanized nail or right-angle screw hook to act as a lock nail.

This birdhouse does not need a roof when mounted directly under the eaves or overhang of a flat-roofed home. In fact it is better without it—young birds need air circulation in warm weather. The locking device on the back of this box makes the birdhouse slip down into place when it is mounted, creating a gap of ½ to ¾ in. between the top edge of the box and the underside of the eaves. If, however, you mount the box outside on a baffled post, you will need to make a roof and provide a gap at the top for air circulation. We'll take care of both situations here.

5. Cut a piece of hardware cloth to lay over the top of the almost finished house. Fasten the hardware cloth around the edges with staples.

6. From a solid piece of ¾-in. straight-grained wood, cut a strip 12 in. long and ½ in. thick. Plane the ¾-in. thickness down to ⅝ in., then bevel ⅛ in. off the ½-in. thickness.

7. Drive 2 nails part way into the back (or top) edge of the roof, ¼ in. from the edge. Align the strip underneath so that it is an equal distance from either edge, then drive the nails part way through it.

8. Position the roof over the house so the back edge is flush with the back of the house and so there is an equal overhang on either side. Then drive the nails part way in. Drive 2 more nails into the front (or bottom) edge of the roof. Then drive all the nails all the way in.

D. 1. You are now ready to mount the house on a post, 2 ft. of which is set in concrete. Center and nail a temporary block of wood

Angle strip • Roof • 10 • 14 • 8¼ • 12 • Hardware cloth • Back • Front • Nail hinge • Left side (door)

C.

to the post, 7 in. down from the top and at right angles to the post. Center and mark a vertical line on the block. On the bottom of the box, center and mark another vertical line, extending toward the front about 2 in.

2. Place the box on the post, resting it on the block. Match up the lines underneath. While holding the box in this position, reach inside the open door and pencil a mark on the post by circling inside the ½-in. holes at the back.

3. Remove the box and lightly drive a 1½-in. galvanized roofing nail into the center of each of the penciled circles. Next to the 2 nails, place a piece of scrap that is ⅝ in. deep to use as a guide. Drive the nails delicately until their heads are just above the depth of the sample block. (If the nail head bends, pull it out and try another.) If the nails stick out farther than that, the box will not be stable and flush against the post. If the nails go in any farther, they will not protrude far enough to go into the lock holes on the box.

4. Slip the box over both nail heads, jiggle it, and pull downward into the lock slots.

D.

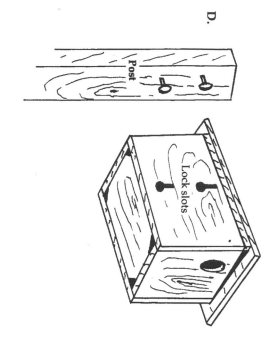

5. Mount your birdhouse on an outside wall just as you would on a post, except that you need to remove the roof and fit the house tightly under the eaves. Or, if there are exposed rafters, mount it beneath the overhang (which is usually 2 in. by 8 in.). You can mark nail locations by pressing the back of the box against a rafter, with the screened top snug against the underside of the eaves at the outer edge of the overhang. The box will conform to the roof slant and angle downward, but don't worry—birds won't mind. Avoid trying to make it level. That will open a gap above, inviting some species to nest on top of the box.

Suggestions

Here are a number of things worth considering as you try for swallows with a birdhouse of this type:

1. Build several—even half a dozen are not too many.

2. Plan on a number of locations: eight to ten feet above the ground on posts—out in the open and away from trees—or under the eaves or overhang, and on several sides of the house. This will help increase acceptance of your birdhouses.

3. Establish a number of alternate locations under the eaves, and switch birdhouses to these spots the moment swallows display interest.

4. Place your houses so that swallows cannot easily see the entrance of the house next door.

5. Do not rush the swallow season. Wait until they flutter around the place, especially under the eaves as if searching. Put up your birdhouses then and you will have more swallows nesting and less trouble from other species.

6. If you put up a birdhouse beneath the overhang on an exposed beam, place a piece of plywood, painted white, on the roof directly above. This is especially effective if the roof has a raised gutter. It allows air space beneath and creates a sun shield, which helps keep down the temperature below.

7. Take down the houses as soon as you are sure that the young ones are gone. Then clean out the nests and replace the housing.

Bottom Entry Swallow House

If your efforts begin to attract swallows, you may have trouble with house sparrows taking over the birdhouses. It's a common problem among birdhouse landlords.

One day I read in the newspaper that swallows in a West Coast city had escaped sparrow harassment by building nests in down-turned overflow pipes atop business buildings. What an idea! Minutes later I was fashioning two houses with bottom entries, 2½ inches in diameter (the average for overflow pipe). When I put the house up, swallows swarmed about, fussed at the entrance, and after proper inspection were shooting up through the hole like feathered bullets. Occasionally a sparrow bumbled beneath in puzzlement.

Unfortunately, I left the birdhouses up all winter. I was horrified to discover that during those months the house sparrows had practiced, learning how to gain entry. The following season was a holy terror. Nothing seemed to work against the sparrows. Cleaning out the eggs and relocating the house proved the best deterrent. The swallows usually found the house first, moved in, raised a brood, and left before the sparrows wised up.

Starlings, too, can be a problem if they nest in your area, but you can minimize the difficulty by taking certain measures suggested at the end of this chapter and in the chapter about predators. This bottom entry house also offers some protection against certain winged predators.

Materials

One-inch boards (actual thickness is ¾ in.) are suggested for the sides, back, and front of this house because there will be a deep bevel. One-inch boards are easier to plane than plywood. However, you can use ⅝-in. plywood if your plane is sharp—but be sure to make the sides 9½ in. long instead of 9¾ in. Spacer blocks must be made from 1-in. boards.

Boards, 1 in., 10 by 2 in.:
Sides (2)—each 9¾ (9½ in. if using ⅝-in. plywood) by 5 in.
Back—8¼ by 7¼ in.
Front—6¼ by 7¼ in.
Spacer blocks (2)—each 1½ by 10 in.

Cedar boards or exterior plywood, ⅝ in., 26 by 16 in. (if 1-in. boards are used as listed above) or 26 by 21½ in. (if ⅝-in. plywood is used for back, sides, and front as well as for parts listed here); or T 1-11 siding scraps:

Bottom—7¼ by 8½ in.
Roof, left side—12 by 8⅝ in.
Roof, right side—12 by 8 in.
Starling block (optional)—plywood, ¼ in., 5 by 5 in.
Sunshade (2 parts)—pegboard (masonite), ¼ in., each 10 by 14 in.
Sunshade cleat—wood, 1 by 1 by 14 in.
Scrap garden hose, 1 short length
Fourpenny galvanized box nails
Caulking compound
Magnetic lock and screws
Butt hinges (2), ½ in., with screws ½ in. long and ³⁄₁₆ in. in diameter
Galvanized box nails (4), 2½ in. long
Screws (4),1¼ in. long
Bolts (2), 3 in. long, ⅜ in. in diameter
Washers (2)
Wing nuts (2) or hexagonal nuts (2)
Mounting block—wood, 1 by 6 by 18 in.
Post—2 in. by 4 in. by 10 ft. (with added-on predator baffle)
(note: Can also use galvanized pipe with a pipe-flange mounting)
Prepared sand-mix concrete, 1 sack

Tools

Square
Ruler
Rasp
Plane
Screwdriver
Brace, with 2½-in. expansion bit, or keyhole saw
Pencil
Saw
Straightedge
Hammer

Instructions

A. 1. Using a square, lay out the parts and cut them according to the dimensions shown. Be sure to cut the corners back ½ in. on the bottom piece.

2. Mark the 2½-in. entry on the bottom piece by first centering a line down the 8½-in. length of the panel. Make a cross mark, 2¾ in. back from the front edge. Center the hole on the cross mark and cut it out with a 2½-in. expansion bit, or use a keyhole saw after drilling a ½-in. hole near what will become the perimeter of the entry. Nail a piece of old garden hose around the entrance on the inside.

A.

Bottom Entry Swallow House

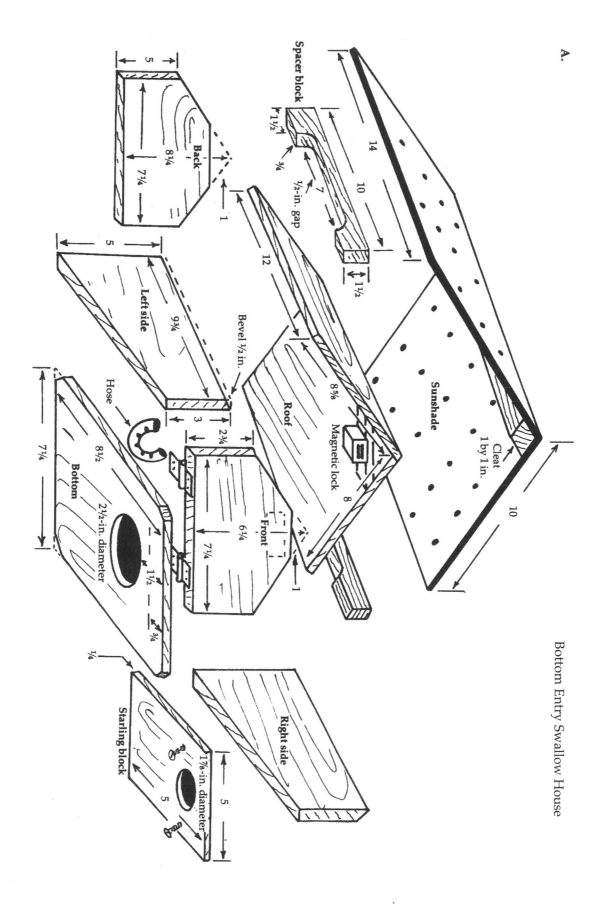

3. If starlings try to invade this house, you may need to construct a starling block. On a 5 by 5-in. piece of ¼-in. plywood, draw a centered vertical line 2⅜ in. from 1 edge. Measure 1⁄16 in. from the same edge and mark an X. Lining up with this mark, use a 1⅞ in. expansion bit or a keyhole saw (as you did in Step A 2) to cut out a 1⅞-in. hole. Smooth the edges with a rasp. When the block is in place, it will clear the butt hinges. (To learn how to use the starling block, refer to the second precaution listed at the end of this chapter.)

6. Lay the 2 roof pieces in place, the wider one overlapping, but flush with the surface of the other. Check the fit and make any needed adjustments.

7. Slide the joined roof pieces until they are flush with the back panel. On the smaller half of the roof, mark 2 position lines— where the roof touches the side corner of the back panel and at the cut-off corner toward the top. Underneath the front and back of the roof, extend the marks 1¼ in. inward, and parallel to the bottom edge. of the roof, from both the front and back edges. Place a cross mark 1¼ in. from the front and back edges to indicate equal overhang.

8. Slide the smaller half of the roof down the slope until the edges of the front and back are visible, then line up 2 nails to connect with the front and back pieces 3 in. down from the roof's top edge. Adjust to the position marks, check for equal overhang, then tack the nails to hold. Lay on the other half to check for fit, making adjustments if needed. Tack one more nail in back, toward the lower corner of the smaller roof half.

9. To seat the roof joint, run a ribbon of caulking compound along the top edge of the smaller roof half. Place 2 nails into the back panel through the larger half, but do not drive the nails all the way in. Set one nail into each side and 3 along the roof joint. Check everything for alignment. Except for those in the front panel, drive in all the nails. Remove the others and slip the front panel out.

10. Lay the front panel down on a piece of ¾-in. scrap with the top, cut-off portion of the panel flush to the edge of the scrap piece. Marking the scrap piece, extend lines 1½ in. down the slope from the top edge of the front piece. Now remove the front panel, and connect the bottom ends of the lines you have just drawn on the scrap piece.

11. Saw out this piece and nail it inside the roof, positioned as a stop when the door is vertical. Angle a nail into the bottom of the block near each end in such a manner that you can swing the hammer from outside the opening to hit the block.

B. 1. Set the bottom panel—weather surface down—on the work-bench, pushing the back edge of the bottom piece against the wall. Put each side piece on a 2-in. block. Be sure the sides have the slanted edge underneath. (The top edge runs at right angles to the front and back ends.) Place the bottom, back, and front in position, weather surface out, just as if they were nailed together.

2. Slip a straightedge along the roof slant of the front, to mark the angle of bevel on each of the side pieces. It will be about ½ in., or ⅜ in. if the sides were ⅝ in. thick. Bevel the sides, being sure that the angles slope in the right direction. Check the bottom piece and mark the slight angle of bevel front and back, then bevel about ⅛ in. Also bevel ⅛ in. off the bottom of the front and back panels so they conform to the upward slant of the bottom piece.

3. Start 2 nails at the bottom of the back panel. Set the bottom in place, allowing ¼ in. of the back panel to extend below the bottom panel. Drive the nails part way in.

4. Start 2 nails in a side, along the back edge. Place the end of the side flush with the back panel and tack to hold. Put a nail toward the front and into the bottom, checking to make sure that approximately ¼in. of the side panel drops below the bottom panel. Drive in the nail. Repeat with the other side. You may have to spring the bottom into alignment before driving the nail into the bottom near the front. Now drive in all the nails.

5. Place the front panel in position and nail temporarily along the bottom but not on the sides. These nails will later be pulled, after the roof is on.

Bottom Entry Swallow House

B.

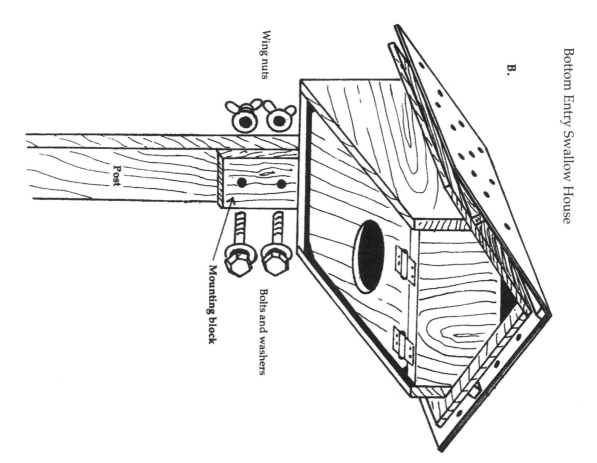

Wing nuts

Post

Mounting block

Bolts and washers

12. Center the magnetic portion of the lock beneath this piece, then screw it on, but not too tight.

13. Set the front panel flush with the bottom. Mark the holes for the butt hinges and install them, temporarily, using only 2 screws for each hinge. Test the door to be sure it opens easily. If it sticks, mark the place, remove the door, and plane it down.

14. To position the metal striker plate on the front panel, put a drop of caulking compound on the magnet and close the door to mark the place. Wipe the material from the magnet, set the plate directly over the mark left on the door, then adjust the magnet to make complete contact. Now tightly set the screws on the magnet and the butt hinges.

15. Now for the sunshade. Although you may leave it off, you will then increase the young swallows' discomfort during hot weather. To make the sunshade, nail the top edge of half the pegboard to the 1 by 1 by 14-in. wood cleat. Now, nail on the other half of the pegboard to form a roof shape.

16. Drill a hole through the top of each spacer block, 1 in. back from each end. (Drilling holes will prevent the wood from splitting when you drive in the nails.) Place 1 block on the roof so that its upper edge is just below the point where, underneath, the roof joins the bottom side of the bevel. At this point, you can drive the 2½-in. box nails into the wall with less likelihood of their going into the inside of the house. (The nails must not stick through). Repeat with the other spacer block.

17. Using fourpenny nails for each corner, nail the sunshade to the spacer blocks.

18. Using 4 screws, fasten a 1 by 6 by 18-in. mounting block to the back of the birdhouse so that the board extends below the house. Be sure the screws do not come through to the inside.

19. Use bolts, washers, and nuts to fasten the house to a baffled post, 2 ft. of which is set in concrete.

Suggestions

The Bottom Entry Swallow House works best when you mount it on a post out in the open and take the following precautions:

1. The entry must be 2½ inches in diameter. If it is too large, the house sparrows may use it. If it is too small, the swallows' wings will get battered as they fly in and out. (An exception is the starling block entrance hole mentioned below.) The entry should be just forward of center to provide nesting space, and the edges should be left rough to allow the swallow to cling while inspecting the interior. Inside, the backward slanting floor and balustrade (the piece of garden hose) help to keep the young ones from falling out.

2. Starlings are readily attracted to the 2½-inch opening of the Bottom Entry Swallow House. Since starlings are early nesters, they can already be occupying nest sites by the time swallows and other migratory species arrive. To discourage starlings from entering this house, construct a block with a 1⅞-in. entrance (see Step A2 of Bottom Entry Swallow House instructions). Remember to remove it just before the young swallows are ready to fly. After the youngsters solo the first few times, the parents like to coax them inside for the night. The larger opening is easier for the fledglings to negotiate.

3. It's not necessary to paint your swallow houses. Painted houses look pretty, but white may be the only color that serves to make houses more attractive to the birds. Natural wood is fine. (If you must paint, use a water-base, exterior latex brand and let the painted house fully dry before mounting it.)

4. The house should be 8 feet from the ground. Avoid placing the post near shrubs, tree limbs, porch railings, telephone wires, or the transverse arm of a downspout from which predators can gain access. Besides, baby swallows need plenty of diving distance when teased into tumbling from the nest by parents offering juicy insects.

5. Keep your swallow houses widely separated. Try one by the side of your house, one in front, and another at the back of the lot. Tree and violet-green swallows have a strong territorial sense and will not nest too close to each other unless, as said before, they cannot see the entrance of their neighbor's house.

6. Place your swallow house with care. Plan on there being droppings underneath. Moreover, when feeding the young, parents keep the nest clean by carrying away the feces in little white sacks (probably made of swallow spit). These are dropped twenty to fifty feet, in a direct line away from the post. Aim the swallow house to avoid these "bomblets" being dropped on your favorite lawn chair or you.

7. Do not leave your swallow houses up all winter! This only gives the house sparrows a chance to practice. Set the houses up around mid-April, or even later, when the swallows show up around mid-April, or even later, when the swallows show demand by fluttering under the eaves. Take the birdhouse down as soon as the young have flown—around mid-July in the case of violet-green swallows. They usually raise only one brood in cities. In the case of tree swallows, watch and wait. They normally raise two broods

8. Minimize the risk of gathering nest materials. Parent swallows hate to land on the ground to pick up nest materials, because it makes them vulnerable to predators. To help out the prospective parents, scatter white feathers, small bits of cotton, and very short pieces of dried grass down the center of your lawn. Never mind worried glances from the neighbors, the swallows will reward you with a show of acrobatic excellence, sizzling across your yard and snatching material off the grass in midflight. In some instances, swallows even have been known to snatch feathers held loosely between a person's fingers. Give it a try. Who knows? One day your neighbors, too, may be sprinkling little white things across their lawns at swallow time.

Purple Martin Houses

Centuries ago Native Americans of the southeastern United States strung gourds on poles to provide purple martins with nesting sites. White settlers continued the practice, which resulted in many communities having large colonies of martins nesting each season.

The largest of our swallows, purple martins are about eight inches long. Wintering in the Amazon basin, they spend their summers from central Mexico north to southern Canada, arriving in the United States from mid-January on. They normally raise four to five young, with each parent feeding the little ones with insects they catch in midair.

Nearly everyone marvels at the complexity of the apartment-

Purple martins are almost totally dependent on human-supplied housing, whether it is traditional gourd houses, or the usual nest box style.

type birdhouses designed for purple martins in the Midwest and East. Some houses have several hundred units! On the West Coast, however, martins are less common, and, although they are of the same species as the East Coast martins, they prefer natural cavity housing to eastern-style apartment facilities. Having lived in woodpecker holes in widely scattered snags, usually near water, they have not had the generations of practice in "close togetherness" living that their more easterly relatives have had.

This may change, though. Some people recently have discovered that martins of the Northwest will accept "trio-unit" houses, which have a single entrance on each of three sides.

Trio-Unit Martin House

If you are seriously into the birdhouse landlord business and purple martins have been seen in your area, try luring prospective tenants into this appealingly small apartment house. Although not ornate in the Hansel and Gretel gingerbread style, the trio unit is serviceable and should last for years.

Materials

Cedar planks, pine, or exterior plywood, ⅝ in., 41½ by 31¼ in.; or T 1-11 siding scraps:

Bottom—19¼ by 9 in.
Sides (2) each 10¼ by 8 by 9 in.
Back—19¼ by 9 in.
Front—19¼ by 7¾ in.
Roof—23 by 13 in.
Dividers (2)—each 9 by 7⅝ by 6¾ in.
Porches (3)—each 6 by 2½ in.

Fourpenny galvanized box nails
Right-angle screw hooks (4), about 1½ in. long
Caulking compound
Mounting block—straight-grained wood, 1 by 8 by 15 in.
Screws (4), 1¼ in.
Post—4 in. by 4 in. by 12 ft.; or galvanized pipe, 1½ or 2 in., 12 ft. long, or longer if house is to be over water (see Step G 2), with threaded pipe flange. Don't forget the post- or pole-mounted predator baffle (See "Predators and Competitors" starting on page 72)
Prepared sand-mix concrete (optional), 1 sack

Tools

Square
Pencil
Ruler
Saw
Plane
Brace, with 2-in. expansion bit or keyhole saw
Drill, with assorted small bits
Compass or 2-in. jar lid
Rasp
Hammer
Screwdriver

Instructions

A. 1. Using a square and a pencil, mark out all the parts, following the dimensions in the exploded drawing. If you are using exterior plywood, remember to work on the weather surface of the material.

2. The 2 side panels should be marked out to join at a common line along the 8-in. dimension, forming a shallow V along the top edges. When you lay the sides out this way, you will have no trouble cut-

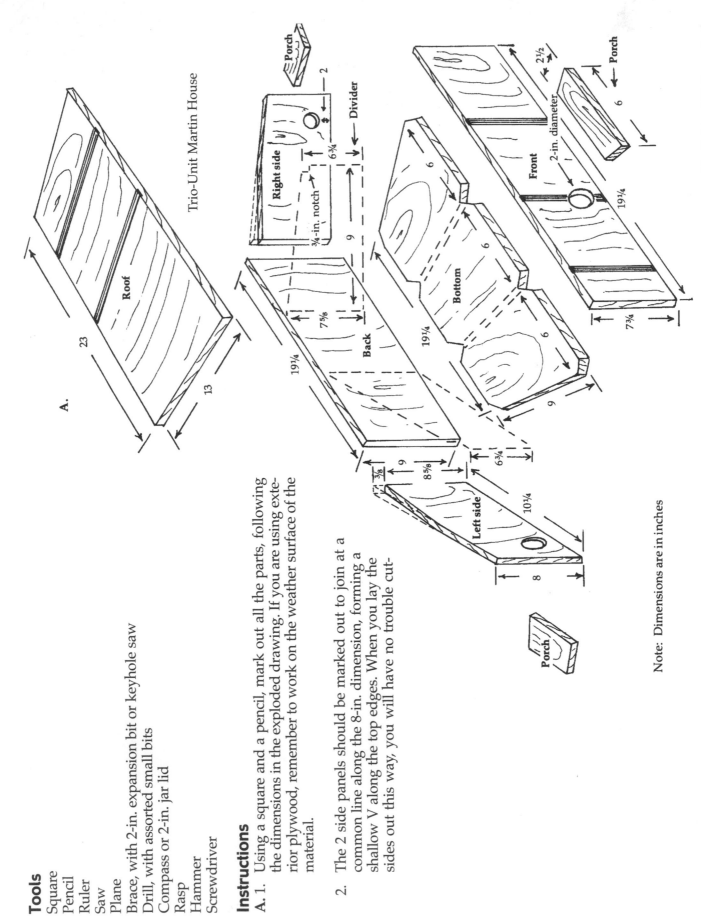

Trio-Unit Martin House

Note: Dimensions are in inches

ting them so they will fit into position, weather side out. (Trust me—it works.) To provide air vent space, drop down ⅜ in. at the 9-in. side of the panel and mark a line at right angles to the back edge, intersecting the slant.

3. Double-check all the measurements, then saw out all the parts and mark them for identification. For your own comfort, plane off the splinters along the sawed edges. (You don't need to sand them.) Be sure to notch each divider, ¾ in. at the top front corner. Cut the corners of the bottom panel back ¾ in.

4. On the back panel's interior surface, draw a horizontal line ⅛ in. down from the top and bevel.

5. On the front panel, weather surface up, mark a vertical line, 8 in. in from the left and extending 4 in. up from the bottom. Put a cross mark 3 in. up.

6. On the left side panel, weather surface up, mark a vertical line, 2⅛ in. in front of the right edge and extending 4 in. up from the bottom. Put a cross mark 3 in. up. Repeat with the right side panel, measuring from the left edge. Draw a vertical line 4 in. up and put a cross mark at 3 in. Repeat with the right side panel.

7. The cross marks made in steps 5 and 6 are the center marks for the 2-in. entrances of the house. Cut them out with a 2-in. expansion bit, but test first on scrap material to make sure the hole will be exactly 2 in. (You may also cut entrances with a keyhole saw if it is sharp. With a compass or jar lid, center and draw a 2-in. circle. Drill a ½-in. opening just inside the circumference. Start the saw there and cut out the larger opening.) Slightly round off the edges of the holes with a rasp.

8. On the bottom piece (inside surface), make a mark 6 in. in from the left, and another 6 in. in from the right. Draw a line through the marks, extending back to front at right angles. (Your dividers will go on the inside of these lines, which should make a central compartment, 6 in. wide.)

9. On the left side of the right-hand line, place a ⅝-in. piece of

wood on edge. Saw a line along its left side, and remove the piece of wood. On the bottom piece, mark the center between these 2 lines 1 in. from the back and front edges. Along the front and back edges, place a mark 1 in. from each side of the center lines. Connect the marks. Cut a right-angle notch into the edge at each point. Repeat for the left side of the bottom piece, but place divider outline and center marks to the right of the line. Now turn the bottom piece over.

B.

Trio-Unit Martin House

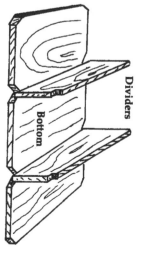

Dividers

Bottom

C.

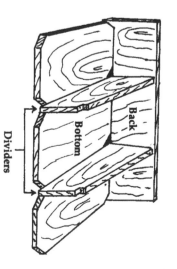

Dividers

Back

Bottom

Dividers

3. Align the dividers to match the perpendicular lines up the back, hold, and drive a nail part way in near the top of each divider. Check for alignment. Set 3 nails along the bottom edge and drive them all in. Now turn the unit upside down and drive in the nails on the bottom panel. Finish driving in those in the back panel.

D. 1. Before you put on the sides, use 2 nails to set the porch blocks under the entrances, flush with the front edges and 1 in. up from the bottom.

2. Start 2 nails at the back of a side panel. Fit the piece flush with the back edge, then nail part way in. Start a nail at the bottom, toward the front (beneath the porch block). Check the bottom. If it has sprung, draw it into place, hold, and drive the nail in, along with the others.

Now is the time to decide if you want to install baffle walls to ward off predators. Refer to the "Predators and Competitors" chapter to learn about baffles. Then, if you want to install them, follow the assembly instructions given there.

E.

F.

Trio-Unit Martin House

D.

B. 1. Start 4 nails through the bottom, each ½ in. in from the notch corners. Set 1 divider on its back edge at a right angle to the workbench, its corner against the wall, and lay the bottom panel against it. Make adjustments to center the notches over the edge of the divider. Drive the nails part way in. Put the other divider in place and nail. Leave all 4 nails sticking out ¼ in. or less.

C. 1. Put the back in position, its bottom edge extending ¼ in. below the bottom panel. Inside, run a short pencil line along the back panel where each divider meets it. Make a short mark where the bottom piece meets the back panel as well. Extend the marks up and to the sides to outline divider and bottom locations. Make these same marks on the outside of the back panel so you can tell where to position the nails. Start 2 nails, 1 for each divider, near the bottom.

2. With the back in position, place the unit on the bench, front against the wall, and slip slats beneath the bottom to hold that ¼-in. drop for the back. Drive the nails part way into the edges of the dividers.

G.

Trio-Unit Martin House

E. 1. On the front panel, which will be the door to the house, use 2 nails to set the porch block 1 in. up and centered beneath the hole.

2. Position the front, planing the edges if the fit is too tight. (The door should swing freely when the hinges are in place.) Place a nail through the right and left side panels so that the nails go through the front panel, ½ in. from the top edge, as shown. There should be ¼ in. between the top of the door and the roof when it is in place. Test by pulling the front open from the bottom. Exchange the hinge nails for right-angle screw hooks. The door is removable, so you can install baffles later if you change your mind about needing them. The advantage of this door is that it exposes all 3 units at once for quick inspection. To lock it at the bottom, drill a small hole into the lower end of each side edge, then insert screw hooks into each hole.

F. 1. Place the roof flush with the back—with an equal overhang on each side—and check the fit. Before nailing, run a strip of caulking compound along the back beveled edge to make the house waterproof. Along the back edge of the roof, set 3 nails part way in, to hold. Drive in 2 more, 1 on each side toward the front. Check it once more and drive the nails in.

G. 1. For mounting on a snag or 4 by 4-in. post (2 ft. of which is set in concrete), cut a mounting block 15 in. long and 8 in. wide. Attach this to the back with 4 screws, allowing the board to extend a few inches above and below the birdhouse. In this way, it can be bolted or nailed securely from above and below.

2. If, instead, you mount the house on a 1½- or 2-in. galvanized pipe, forget the mounting block and center a threaded pipe flange beneath the bottom of the house, then securely fasten it with screws. If you want the house near water, set 2 ft. of the 12-ft. pole in concrete. If you want the house over water, be sure the pipe is long enough to extend 6 ft. above the surface after the pipe is driven into the bottom. If nest box predators such as snakes and raccoons are present in your area, a pole-mounted baffle will help to protect the nest and house.

Six Compartment Martin House

If you are fortunate enough to live where martins readily take to multiplex units, you can build this relatively simple, six compartment house and expect to have some martins residing in it. Although not light in weight, this house is inexpensive and rugged.

Materials

Cedar boards, or exterior plywood, ⅝ in., 4 ft. by 4 ft.8¾ in.; or T 1-11 siding scraps:

Compartment section:

Bottom—19¼ by 18⅝ in.
Single-entry sides (2)—each 19⅞ by 7 in.
Double-entry sides (2)—each 19¼ by 7 in.
Center divider—19¼ by 6 in.
Cross dividers (2)—each 18⅝ by 6 in.
Single-entry porch blocks (2)—each 6 by 2½ in.
Double-entry porch blocks (2)—each 12 by 2½ in.

Top section:

Sides (2)—each 19⅞ by 2 in.
Ends (2)—each 19¼ by 6 by 2 in.
Roof, left side—23⅞ by 14⅝ in.
Roof, right side—23⅞ by 14 in.

Fourpenny galvanized box nails
Ceiling—plywood, ¼ in., 19¼ by 18⅝ in.
Right-angle screw hooks (8),1¼ in. long
Ceiling cleats (8)—straight-grained wood, 1 by 1 by 24 in., ripped in half to make each cleat 1 by ½ by 6 in.
Small box nails (16), 1 in. long
Lock blocks (2)—wood, each 3 by 2 in.
Galvanized hardware cloth, ⅛-in. mesh, 13 by 6 in.
Staples, #5, wire brad
Brads (4), ½ in.
Caulking compound
Screen-door hooks and eyes (4 pairs)
Eye screws (optional), ⅜ in. in diameter inside
Perch (optional)—⅜-in. wooden dowel, 24 in. long
Mounting block—wood, 2 by 6 in., 12 to 16 in. long
Screws (2), 4 in. long and at least ¼ in. in diameter
Post—4 in. by 4 in. by 15 ft. (Don't forget the predator baffle!)
Wood, 2 in. by 6 in. by 11 ft.
Wood, 4 by 4 by 30 in.

Wood, 2 by 4 by 33 in.
Plywood, ¼ in., 6 by 30 in.
Carriage bolts (3), 7 in, long, ⅜ in. in diameter
Nuts (3)
Washers (6)
Sixteen-penny galvanized nails (9)
Sixteen-penny duplex nails (2), double heads
Wood preservative, 1 pint
Prepared sand-mix concrete, 2 sacks

Tools

Square
Pencil
Ruler
Saw
Brace, with2 ¾-in., 2-in, 1¾-in., and-½-in. expansion bits, and screwdriver bit or keyhole saw
Chisel (optional)
Hammer
Plane
Pliers
Brace, with ⅜- and 1-in. bits
Scrap board, straightedge, 8 ft. long
Shovel or post-hole digger
Scrap boards (2), 1 in. by 4 in., 8 to 10 ft. long
Stakes (2), 2 by 2 in.
String, 8 ft. long
Plumb bob or old spark plug
Tenpenny duplex nails (4), double heads

Instructions

A. 1. This house is built in 2 sections. Start by laying out all the pieces for the compartment (lower) section, penciling the configurations on the weather surface according to the dimensions shown. Check everything twice. (The grain need not run vertically on the walls; if you use T 1-11 siding, plan your layout so that the grooves in the material can be tucked under the roof extension.) It will help if you lay out the sides exactly alike, weather surface out and entrances offset in the same direction. When assembled, the sides will then go into correct position.

Six Compartment Martin House

A.

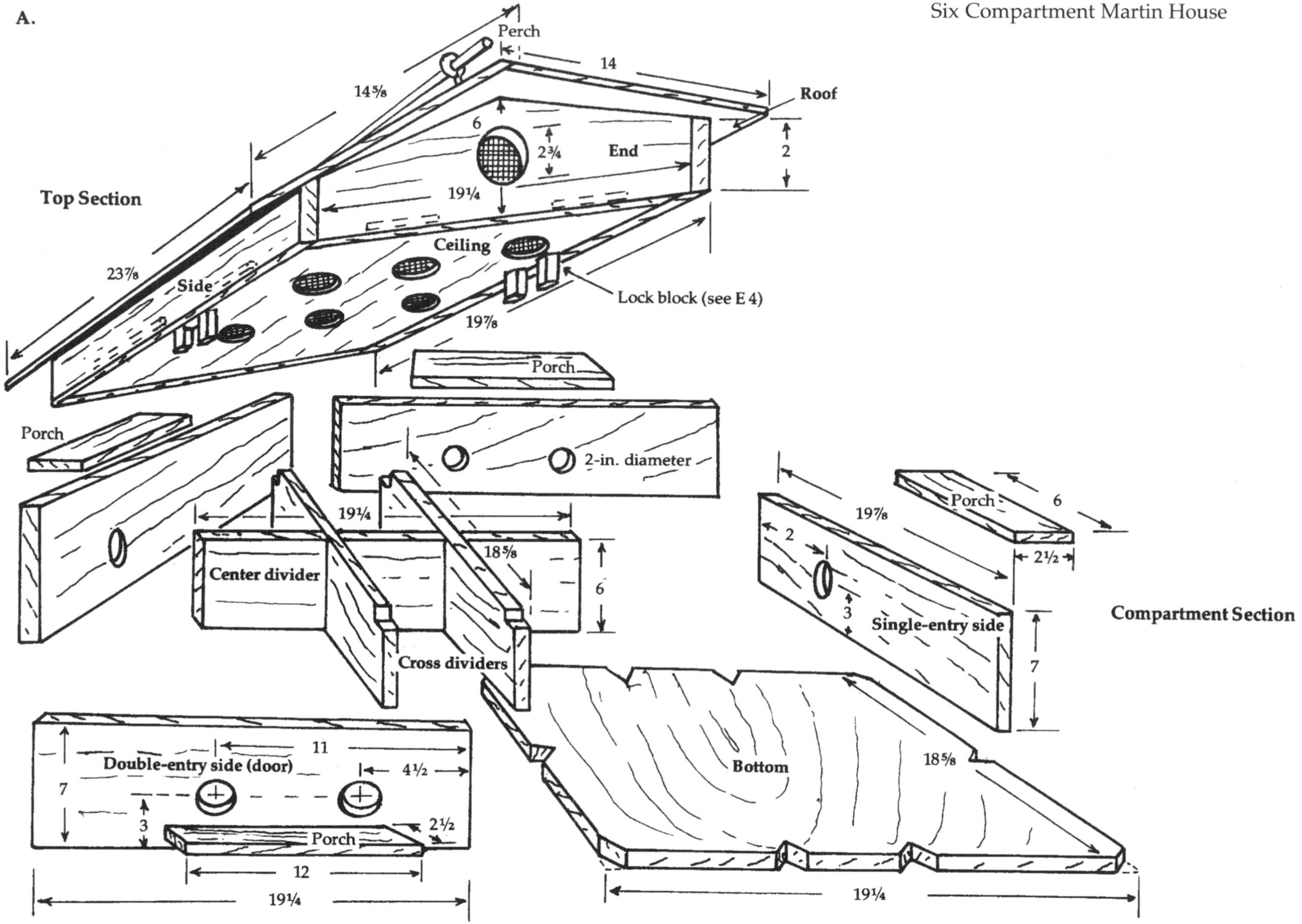
Top Section
Perch
14
Roof
14⅝
6
2¾
End
2
19¼
Ceiling
23⅞
Side
Lock block (see E 4)
19⅞
Porch
Porch
2-in. diameter
19¼
18⅝
Center divider
6
Cross dividers
19⅞
Porch
6
2
2½
3
Single-entry side
7
Compartment Section
11
Double-entry side (door)
4½
7
3
2½
Porch
12
19¼
Bottom
18⅝
19¼

Note: Dimensions are in inches

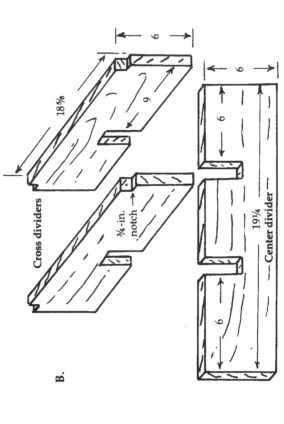

B.

Cross dividers

Center divider

Note: Dimensions are in inches

2. To get the correct entrance centers, draw a 12-in. horizontal line on the weather surface of the 19¼-in. (double-entry) sides, 3 in. up from the bottom. Measure 4½ in. in from the right. Draw a vertical line to intersect the horizontal line. Now, measure in 11 in. from the right and draw another vertical line to intersect the horizontal line.

3. On the weather surface of the 19⅞-in. (single-entry) panels, draw a 3-in. horizontal line 3 in. up from the bottom. Measure in 2 in. from the right. Draw a vertical line to intersect the other line.

4. Saw out all panels, except the dividers, of the bottom section. Drill the entrance holes with a 2-in. expansion bit.

B. 1. To make divider notches for the "egg crate" assembly, take the 19¼-in. center divider. On the top edge, make 2 marks, each one 6 in. in from the left and right. Extend each vertically, 3 in. from the top edge. At the bottom of each line, make a ⅝-in. horizontal line toward the center of the divider. Lay the edge of a piece of scrap wood ⅝ in. deep along one 3-in. line, toward the center of the board. Draw a line against the scrap piece, paralleling the vertical line. Repeat on the other side. The notches should be 6 in. apart on the inside.

2. On the 2 cross dividers, measure in 9 in. from the left and right, then mark. Draw notches as you did for the center divider. There should be 9 in. on each side of the divider notch.

3. Now saw out the 3 divider pieces. Cut the inner notches with a sharp chisel or drill them with a ⅝-in. bit. At the top on each end of the cross dividers, make a ¾-in. notch.

C. 1. Assemble the egg crate and place it on the bottom panel, but do not nail it. Adjust the dividers so the compartments each measure 6 by 9 in. and are flush with the edges of the bottom. On the floor panel, mark 2 in. along both sides of the ends of the dividers. Measure along the edge of the floor, ¾ in. from each of the divider marks. Lift off the egg crate and center a point, 1⅛ in. back from the floor edge in the space to be occupied by each divider. Draw lines connecting the ¾-in. marks on

the edge with this point in order to form a right-angle notch. Saw out the notches. Mark the corners back ¾ in. and saw them off. The notches and corners allow the house to have drainage and light.

2. Tack a nail temporarily at the top of each divider intersection. Turn the unit over and place it on blocks, with the center divider toward you. Place the bottom panel on top, lining up the divider marks underneath with the dividers. Place a scrap board against the end of the bottom and the divider to be sure they are flush. Tack a nail into the divider near the apex of the notch.

3. Carefully lift the unit by the center divider and turn the other end toward you. Adjust and tack with a nail. Turn the unit 90 degrees and adjust it to align with the marks beneath. Tack the 2 dividers. Do the same with the other side. Check the alignment, then drive in all the nails.

4. For extra drainage in the floor, drill one ½-in. hole in the back inner corner of each compartment.

D. 1. Nail the 6-in. porch blocks under the single entries, 1 in. up from the bottom, and flush with the side-panel edges. Center and nail the 12-in. porches beneath the double entrances.

2. Place the bottom assembly on 2 slats, each ¼ in. thick, allowing enough side drop for rain to drip off. Slide the bottom unit against the wall, and place a short, ⅝-in. piece of scrap across the 2 divider ends. Start 2 nails near the bottom of 1 side panel. Place it in position and drive the nails part way in. *Check that the entrance is close to the floor, not up in the air.* Put a nail into the center divider. Nail the other corner and put 2 more nails near the notch. Repeat with the other side.

3. Before going further, let's center the vent openings for the ceiling (of the top section of the house). From ¼-in. plywood, cut a piece 19¼ by 18⅝ in. Lay it over the dividers and mark the compartment corners underneath the ceiling piece by running a pencil along the top edge of the dividers. Draw a line connecting the corners. Drill a 1¾-in. hole for each compartment, centered at the cross marks. Lay the piece aside.

4. The double-entry sides will be the doors you use for inspecting the compartments. Check that the doors fit on both sides. If they are too tight, plane the edges. Place hinge nails ½ in. down from the top on each side, but do not nail them all the way in. This sets the location and makes it easier to exchange the nails for right-angle screw hooks, so the door can be removed to install baffles. (Refer to the "Predators and Competitors" chapter to find out when you need baffles and how you can make them.) Keep your options open. In starling country, you may want to try doors with 1¾-in. openings instead of 2-in. openings. Drill small holes through both ends near the bottom and lock with screw hooks.

E. 1. Now for the top section. Check the drawings and lay out the components, marking dimensions on the weather surface. Saw out the pieces, mark, and lay aside. Halfway down, in the center of each end panel, drill a 2¾-in. hole.

2. Bevel the sides of the top section ¼ in., to fit the roof slope. Check the sides for fit with the front and back panels.

C.

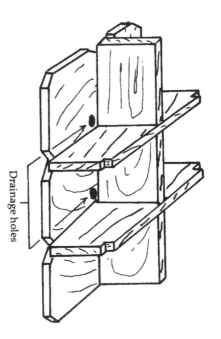

Six Compartment Martin House

Drainage holes

D.

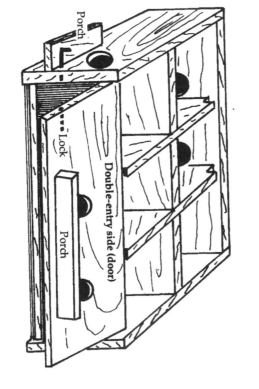

Porch

Lock

Porch

Double-entry side (door)

8. Nail the 2 sides to the front and back pieces, using 2 nails in each corner.

9. Lay the smaller roof section on the top section and check the angle. Bevel off about ½ in. along the top (left) edge of the roof piece. Try the other roof piece, mark, and bevel it to fit with the smaller roof section.

10. The ceiling panel will square up the frame of the roof section. Set 1 edge in place and mark out the notch to cut around each lock block. Make these notches so the fit is as snug as possible. Nail the ceiling in place with 4 brads at an angle, but leave them sticking out ⅛ in. so you can remove them with pliers. Place the unit over the lower section to check the fit and positioning of the lock blocks.

11. Lay the smaller roof section on the top unit, leaving equal overhang at both ends. Tack the section down near the top. Run a strip of caulking compound along the beveled edge to seal the top.

12. Now, position the other roof piece and tack it down near the top. Nail 4 nails, 1 in each bottom corner, part way in. Put another nail into the middle of each side wall. Place 3 nails, evenly spaced, along the top to tighten the caulked seam. Now drive the nails all the way in.

F. 1. Install 4 screen-door hooks and eyes to lock the top and bottom sections together.

2. If you want to, install a perch on the top of the house. In the peak of the roof, drill 2 small holes, each about 1 in. in from the edge. Twist eye screws ½ in. into the wood. Line up the openings. Slide the 24-in. Length of dowel through the eye of 1 of the screws from the inside until it sticks out the end about 2½ in. Now thread it through the other eye, lining it up even with the ends of the roof. If the dowel is too loose, twist the eye screws to wind it.

3. A simple method of mounting this martin house is shown in the drawing. Lift off the top of the house. Underneath the floor

E. Roof sections

Bevel ¼ in.

Bevel ½ in.

14

14⅝

23⅞

19¼

18⅝

Cleats
1 by ½ by 6

Lock block

Hardware cloth

Ceiling,

1¾-in. diameter

18⅝

19¼

3. Saw 8 cleats, 6 in. long from 1 by 1-in. material. They should be ½ in. thick.

4. Cut 2 lock blocks, 2 by 3 in., each with a notch that is ⅝ in. wide and 1 in. deep, centered in the end. Place the notched block over the center divider, next to the wall. Adjust the top, side section in place, mark the position of the block, and nail. Do this with the other block. Clinch the nails on the outside.

5. Lay the cleats flat, ¾-in. surface down, ¼ in. up from the bottom, inside, and near the ends of the 2 sides and the end sections. Do not place them less than 1 in. from the ends. Nail them on, using 1-in. box nails.

6. With a hammer, staple hardware cloth over the holes on the upper side of the ceiling panel surface, clinching the points on the other side.

7. Next, staple hardware cloth over the holes inside the upper end pieces, which will go under the roof. (Do not use ordinary fly screen. Woodpeckers can tear it apart and let in the bees.)

F.

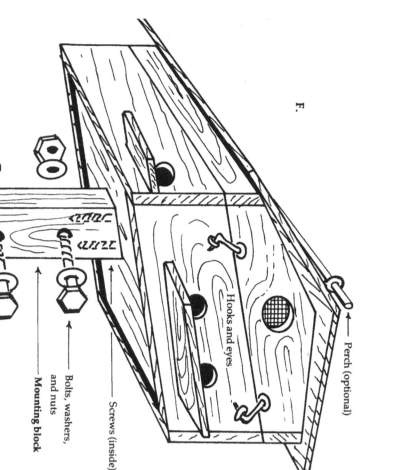

Perch (optional)

Screws (inside)

Hooks and eyes

Mounting block

Bolts, washers, and nuts

Post

of the house, center the mounting block. Screw 2 heavy, 4-in. screws into the block. (It is easiest to use the brace with a screwdriver bit for this.) Clamp the unit to the top of a post (2½ ft. of which is set in concrete), then drill holes for two 5½-in. bolts. Use bolts, nuts, and washers to fasten the house in place.

G. 1. Using the square, draw a line at a right angle across the center of the 2 by 6. Saw it into 2 equal parts, each 66 in.

2. Paint all the pieces with wood preservative. (Work in a well-ventilated area and follow product directions.) Before beginning assembly, allow 24 hours or more for the preservative to soak into the wood and dry.

3. Nail the 2 by 4 to the 4 by 4, flush on one end, 4-in. surfaces together. Three nails, staggered down the length, will do it.

4. Using 3 nails, fasten the 2 by 6 alongside, flush with the 2 you have joined and flush at 1 end.

5. Lay the ¼-in. plywood alongside the opposite surface, then lay the other 2 by 6 on top, flush with 1 end. Fasten it with the 3 remaining nails.

H. 1. Lay the assembly on its side and slip the 4 by 4-in. post into the slot, ½ in. from the bottom. Put a 2-in. block under the other end.

2. Place the straightedge board alongside. Align the 4 by 4-in. post and assembly to conform with the straightedge.

3. Tack the unit together with the 2 duplex nails.

4. Mark the spots for 3 holes. The first should be centered to go through the 4 by 4-in. post, 3 in. up from the bottom; the second should be centered to go through the 4 by 4-in. post, 30 in. above the first. The third should be centered to go through the edge of the 2 by 4 (stop block), 1 in. from its top.

5. With the 1-in. bit, drill at each mark, ⅜ in. in depth. Change to the ⅜-in. bit. Drill each of the holes through the 4 by 4 and both

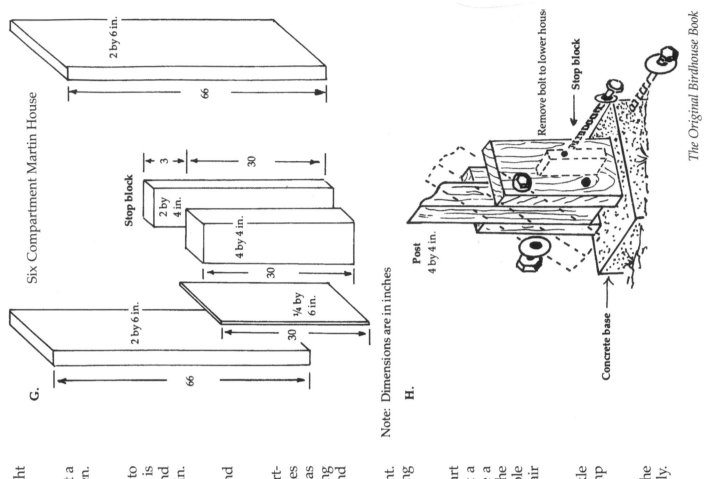

Six Compartment Martin House

Note: Dimensions are in inches

The Original Birdhouse Book

6. 2 by 6s. Make the holes as straight as possible and at a right angle to the assembly.

Press a washer into each hole and run the bolts through. Put a washer and a nut for each bolt on the other side and tighten. Pull out the duplex nails.

7. Outside, pick the location for the post and start digging. Try to keep the hole 8 or 9 in. in diameter. Dig it down to 29 in. If it is too deep, sprinkle a little dirt onto the bottom, tamp down, and measure. The top of the 4 by 4 spreader should be about 1 in. above ground level.

8. Lay out the string, plumb bob, 2 scrap boards, and stakes, and get someone to help.

9. Lift the post assembly and set it into the hole. Have your partner hold it in a vertical position while you drive the stakes about 4 ft. out at 90 degrees from each other with the post as the apex. Tack the ends of the scrap boards to the stakes; using the duplex nails. Lift each board as high as you can reach and tack it to the post on the surface, 90 degrees from the other.

10. Hang the string and plumb bob to check vertical alignment. Make adjustments by pulling the nails, 1 at a time, and tacking them in when the post lines up parallel to the string.

11. If the ground is dry, wet down the hole with a fine mist. Start mixing the concrete in a large pail, adding a little water at a time. The mix should not be soupy, but it should pour like a double thick waffle batter. Keep mixing and pouring until the hole is filled. Between pours, run a long stick down the hole and jiggle it all around the post. This will help to eliminate air pockets. Trowel and shape the surface until it is smooth.

12. Let the concrete cure for a week. In dry, hot weather, sprinkle with a fine mist of water and protect the surface with damp newspapers or wet burlap.

13. To lower the post, have someone hold it while you take out the bottom bolt. Then the two of you can let it down smoothly.

(Some prefer to take out the top bolt for its hinge effect. This allows a bit more leverage. Either way will work.) By bolting the birdhouse to the post, to be raised or lowered, you avoid lots of climbing on unstable ladders for annual cleaning and inspection.

Note: One drawback to this style of nest box pole is that you cannot monitor the boxes during the breeding season without spilling the nest contents around inside each compartment as the post is lowered. Many manufacturers now produce housing poles that permit the housing to be lowered while remaining level. Most of these designs use a pulley system. For more information, contact the Purple Martin Conservation Association—see page 103 for more information.

Suggestions

Here are a few things worth remembering about purple martin houses.

1. Purple martins are flyers, not roadrunners. Equipped with weak feet, they do not hop about effectively, so keep the entrance low, just an inch or two above the floor.

2. While the standard entrance is 2 inches in diameter, martins of the Northwest have been observed using 1¾-inch entrances. The question is, will the starlings? Using removable panels, you can experiment with each size opening.

3. To cut down on your starling problem, you might want to paint the inside of your martin house white. Starlings seem to avoid houses with bright insides. This approach is quite effective, although a *few* starlings in the Northwest have been observed nesting in such houses. Commercial martin houses are currently being manufactured from white-painted aluminum and heavy molded white plastic, both for this reason and because they are lighter and easier to put up. Many even come with crescent-shaped starling-resistant entry holes.

4. Returning home after a hard day of bug chasing, martins seem to enjoy a landing platform near the entry, even though they are capable of clinging to an entrance.

5. Keep the compartments of the trio unit fairly large—six inches wide, nine inches deep. Martins seem to accept these large accommodations more readily than the less roomy compartments of smaller houses. Coupled with an entrance near the floor, their nests remain cleaner and less matted. And there's plenty of romping room for the youngsters!

6. Compartment dividers should be close to the ceiling. When you build the six compartment unit, do not omit the ceiling—fledglings can flip over the dividers. Such behavior is disruptive.

7. Use baffle walls if owls and hawks appear to be a threat (see the chapter "Predators and Competitors").

8. Paint your wooden martin housing white. This reflects sunlight and keeps the house as much as 12 degrees Fahrenheit cooler than an unpainted wood house. A water-base, exterior latex brand is good paint to use.

9. In the Northwest, mount your martin houses six to eight feet high on old snags or pilings, over water, and close to a martin colony. Mount them eight to twelve feet high if the pole is on land, near water. In the Midwest and East, use a post about 15 feet tall. As always, where nestbox predators are present, be sure to use a pole-mounted baffle. Put martin housing up early—in late winter, as a general rule—so you are ready when the first adult male martins return as scouts for the colony, seeking available housing.

Tiny Tenants

Houses for Wrens, Chickadees, Titmice, Nuthatches, and Creepers

Many tiny birds comb out woodlands searching for insects and insect eggs to eat, thus helping to keep forest damage in check. Some of these birds are cavity nesters and will often accept human-made boxes. A few— such as wrens, chickadees, nuthatches, titmice, and brown creepers—may live in your neighborhood or be attracted to your feeders. If so, they are worth the effort it takes to coax them into nesting nearby.

Wrens

Perhaps the most common of these prospective tiny tenants is a diminutive bundle of energy known as the **house wren.** Despite its small size (4¾ inches), its song floods the neighborhood with loud, cascading notes. It can be quickly identified, as it moves in jerks and twitches, by its upthrust tail, buff-colored underparts, brown back, and short, rounded, barred wings.

The house wren's general summer range is across most of southern Canada, south to the western part of South Carolina, Kentucky, southern Missouri, west-central Texas, southern Arizona, and northern Baja California. It winters from South Carolina, the Gulf states, Texas, and California, south to southern Florida and southern Mexico.

The male is a compulsive nest builder, using abandoned woodpecker holes and human-made boxes as nest sites. Moreover, he will often stuff sticks into the entrances of nest boxes nearby, making them useless to larger birds. He may even peck holes in the eggs of other nesting species. Once the female is attracted to the nest, she may throw out his work bit by bit and start over. They often squabble over nest construction, but it gets done. The female then lays six to eight eggs, which are peppered with tiny brown spots. Sometimes the male will coax another female into accepting one of his nests, then help to feed both families—or even the offspring of a different species nesting in the area!

The **Bewick's wren** is an avid insect hunter, searching near buildings or along fences for its favorite food. This friendly creature is about five inches long, wears a distinct, white stripe over its eye, and sports a fan-shaped tail. It may choose to nest in a mailbox, an old fishing creel, an abandoned woodpecker hole, or your birdhouse, where it will lay five to seven brown-spotted eggs.

Wintering along the Gulf Coast to southern Florida, this wren's general summer range is southern British Columbia to southern Utah, southern Ontario, southern Nebraska, southern Michigan, central Pennsylvania, south to Mexico and northern portions of the Gulf states.

Like Bewick's, the nonmigratory **Carolina wren,** which insists on singing year-round, has a distinctive eyebrow stripe but not a fan-shaped tail. About 5¾ inches long, this chunky fellow occurs from Long Island, New York, southern Pennsylvania, and southern Iowa, south to Florida, the Gulf Coast, northern Mexico, and west to eastern Nebraska and central Texas. Its favorite haunts are woodland thickets and brush along streams or rocky, brush-covered slopes.

The Carolina wren favors woodpecker holes, but may also choose an old shoe or bucket in your shed as nesting sites, where four to six white or pinkish, brown-spotted eggs are laid. This may occur as far north as Minnesota or Maine, to which the Carolina wren has pushed its present range, although severe weather may kill off the individuals in the northernmost parts of its range.

Tufted titmice can be enticed to a nest box placed in the proper woodland habitat.

Chickadees

Among the friendliest of all the birds that flock to your feeder are the chickadees. Traveling in loose flocks among the hardwoods or evergreens, they are often attracted to feeding stations by suet, peanut butter, and sunflower seeds. It is even possible to have one feed from your hand, if you have the patience.

The **black-capped chickadee**, around five inches long, has a southern range extending across northern California, northern New Mexico, and the western part of North Carolina. A year-round resident throughout the northern states and Canada, it will live as far north as there are trees. Alighting upside down to scrutinize every inch of bark in its search for spider eggs, cocoons, and other forms of dormant insect life, these birds have a phenomenal capability for winter survival. But this can occur only as long as the food lasts. Otherwise, their little furnaces go out.

Easily identified by the black cap and bib, white underparts and gray backs, they favor old nest cavities or human-made boxes, where they lay six to eight speckled, reddish eggs. Two broods sometimes are raised.

The **chestnut-backed chickadee**, a 4½-inch relative of the black-capped chickadee, ranges through Douglas fir forests of the West and can be easily distinguished by the chestnut color on its back and sides. It, too, favors abandoned woodpecker holes or human-made nest boxes, properly placed on tree trunks that are free of limbs. Nesting habits, nest, and eggs are essentially like those of the black-cap.

The **Carolina chickadee** has markings almost identical to those of its cousin the black-capped chickadee, except that the Carolina's bib has a pronounced break with the white breast. This 4½-inch little tyke ranges from southeast Kansas to central New Jersey, south into central Texas and Florida. An early breeder, it may begin nesting in mid-February, when attracted to natural nest cavities or human-made boxes. It also has similar nesting habits to those of the black-capped, except that it is apt to choose wet woodlands for a location.

Titmice

Another frequenter of forests that feeds on damaging insects is the noisy **tufted titmouse**, which is found from New Jersey, Ohio, Illinois, and Nebraska south to southern Florida, the Gulf Coast, and central Texas. Readily attracted to feeding stations, this six-inch, all gray, crested bird favors hollow trees and sometimes human-made nest boxes, usually near swampy bottomlands. Boldly it will snatch strands of hair from living animals to line its nest, where it lays five to six white eggs.

The species formerly known as the **plain titmouse** is just that—plain and quite gray all over. It is now broken up into two distinct species: the **oak titmouse** (found in western California and Oregon) and the **juniper titmouse** (found in the Southwest from west Texas to Colorado and southeastern Oregon and California). Cousins of the tufted, both are about five inches long and frequent slopes of oak, pine, and juniper in the West. Oak and juniper titmice favor abandoned woodpecker holes or human-made nest boxes, where they lay six to eight eggs. As soon as the young are adept at foraging, the parents encourage them to depart from the home territory.

Nuthatches and Creepers

A black-capped fellow that is 5 or 6 inches long and has a white face and underparts and a gray back is probably a **white-breasted nuthatch**, especially if it insists on inspecting the bark on your trees. If a bird visiting your yard has a black mask across the eyes and reddish underparts, and is about 4½ inches long, then you can identify your visitor as a **red-breasted nuthatch**. The white-breasted nuthatch has a range from southern Canada to southern Mexico; the red-breasted, from southeast Alaska, Newfoundland, and south to southern California and North Carolina. It may winter along the Gulf Coast.

Traveling with chickadees and other birds, picking off insects and larvae, both will readily visit feeding stations, although they will carry some food away, tucking it into bark crevices to save for another time. Both favor woodpecker holes or human-made boxes, where they lay five to eight eggs. The red-breasted may insist on excavating its own nest cavity, however, and may smear pitch around the entrance to deter insects, predators, and nest-site competitors.

Shadowlike, the **brown creeper** often accompanies noisy bands of chickadees and nuthatches. It circles the base of a tree trunk to work upward, then flies to the base of another to do it all over again. Propped on its stiff tail, it uses its downward curving, needle sharp bill to probe crevices for insects. Mottled brown and gray on the back, this five-inch fellow flattens against the tree trunk, hiding its white underparts when danger threatens. Not a frequenter of nest cavities, the little creeper builds a hammock-shaped structure under loose bark, where it lays four eggs.

In the West, creepers can be found from southeast Alaska to Nicaragua; in the East, its range is from Newfoundland to the Appalachians. Winter headquarters are along the Gulf Coast.

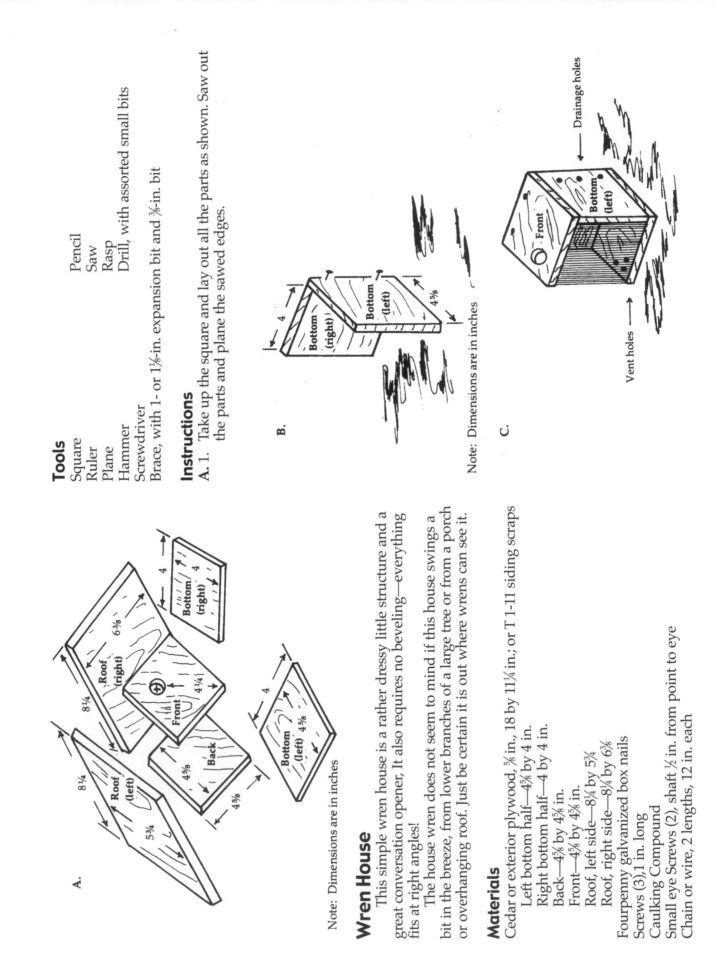

A.

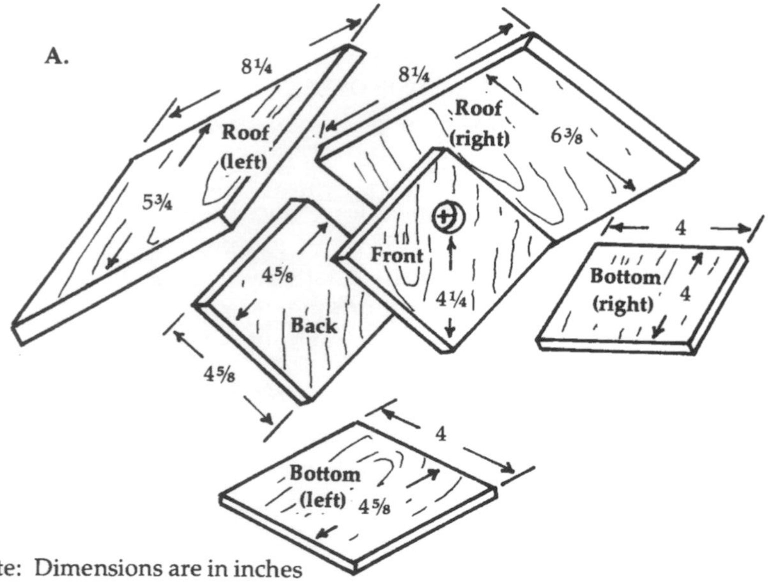
8¼
Roof
(left)
5¾
8¼
Roof
(right)
6⅜
Front
4¼
4⅝
Back
4⅝
4
Bottom
(right)
4
4
Bottom
(left)
4⅝

Note: Dimensions are in inches

Wren House

This simple wren house is a rather dressy little structure and a great conversation opener, It also requires no beveling—everything fits at right angles!

The house wren does not seem to mind if this house swings a bit in the breeze, from lower branches of a large tree or from a porch or overhanging roof. Just be certain it is out where wrens can see it.

Materials

Cedar or exterior plywood, ⅝ in., 18 by 11¼ in.; or T 1-11 siding scraps
- Left bottom half—4⅝ by 4 in.
- Right bottom half—4 by 4 in.
- Back—4⅝ by 4⅝ in.
- Front—4⅝ by 4⅝ in.
- Roof, left side—8¼ by 5¾
- Roof, right side—8¼ by 6⅜

Fourpenny galvanized box nails
Screws (3),1 in. long
Caulking Compound
Small eye Screws (2), shaft ½ in. from point to eye
Chain or wire, 2 lengths, 12 in. each

Tools

Square	Pencil
Ruler	Saw
Plane	Rasp
Hammer	Drill, with assorted small bits
Screwdriver	

Brace, with 1- or 1⅛-in. expansion bit and ⅜-in. bit

Instructions

A. 1. Take up the square and lay out all the parts as shown. Saw out the parts and plane the sawed edges.

B.

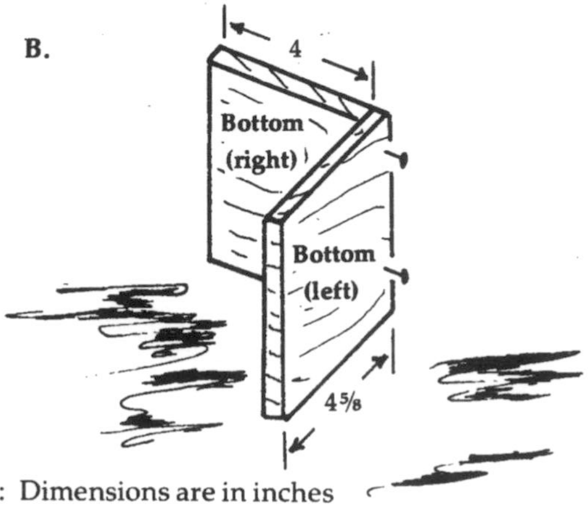
4
Bottom
(right)
Bottom
(left)
4⅝

Note: Dimensions are in inches

C.

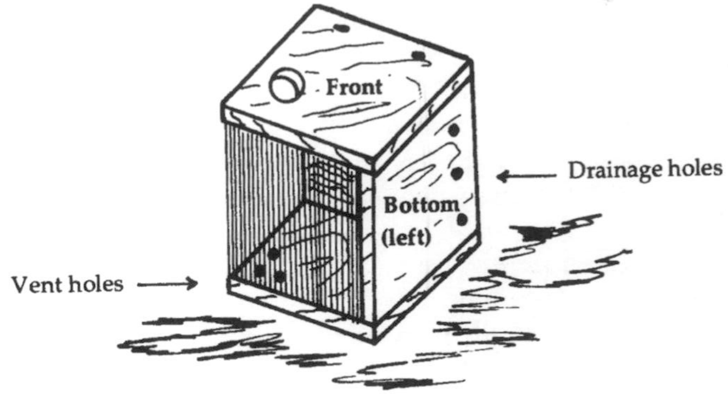
Front
Drainage holes
Bottom
(left)
Vent holes

2. In the front piece, drill a 1-in. entrance, centered as shown in the diagonal, 4¼ in. up from the bottom corner, if this birdhouse is for house or Bewick's wrens. If it is for Carolina wrens, drill a 1⅛-in. hole. Round the edges with a rasp.

B. 1. Begin assembly by putting together the 2 bottom pieces, the larger part overlapping the smaller. Start 2 nails near the edge of the larger (bottom left) piece and join them as shown. Do not nail all the way.

C. 1. On the workbench, lay the larger (left) piece flat, with a scrap board underneath, allowing the smaller (right) piece to hang over the edge of the bench. Drill 3 drain holes, each ⅜ in. in diameter, next to the junction of the 2 pieces.

2. Near the top corner of the back panel, drill 3 vent holes, ⅜ in in diameter. Place the back in position, vent holes at the top, and tack into the edge of the smaller bottom half. If the fit looks good, drive the nails in.

3. Position the front, and tack 2 nails for contact with the edge of the smaller bottom half. Check for alignment, then drive the nails in.

D.

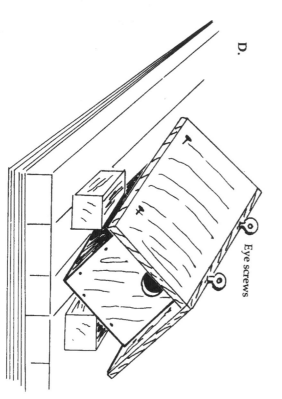

Eye screws

D. 1. Lay the unit down on the small half of the roof panel to measure equal overhang, front and back. Mark the position. Be sure that the temporary nails sticking out of the bottom left panel are toward you, not up.

2. Turn the box over and start 2 nails in the smaller (left) roof section, near the top of the front and back pieces. Align and drive part way to hold.

3. Check the other half of the roof just for fit, then lay it aside. Set 2 more nails in the smaller half, this time near the bottom of the front and back panels. Do not set any nails in the side, which will be removable. If the panels and nails are straight, drive the nails in.

4. Drill a small hole between the 2 temporary nails sticking out from the lower end of the bottom left panel. Drill 2 more holes, 1 in the front panel and 1 in the back panel to connect with the edges of the bottom left piece. Place a screw in each of these 3 holes to fasten the bottom left panel to the house. Remove the 2 nails, using a block under the hammer to avoid pulling off the panel. Galvanized nails are the very dickens to pull. This will be your cleanout door. Be sure not to use it for inspecting the nest when the young are present.

5. Run a ribbon of caulking compound along the top edge of the roof joint. Start 2 nails near the top of the larger (right-hand) roof section, lay it on the house, and drive the nails in, allowing the compound to ooze from the seam. This will seal the house against driving rain. Start 2 more nails lower down, into the end pieces.

6. Place 2 eye screws at each end of the roof peak and use 2 chains or wires to hang the birdhouse 6 to 10 ft. above the ground.

Chickadee–Nuthatch–Titmouse House

Sometimes the high visibility of a birdhouse is more of a detriment than an asset in attracting birds, especially the more timid ones that creep along the bark in search of insects. The unusual house described in the following instructions blends into the landscape and appeals to such tiny tenants as chickadees, nuthatches, titmice, and perhaps even wrens. You just never know. A simple design, it requires only five pieces of wood. Before nailing it to the tree, you attach pieces of bark on the sides and top, making it resemble a large knob on the tree trunk.

Chickadee-Nuthatch-Titmouse House

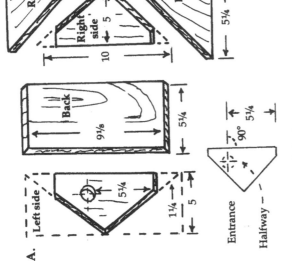

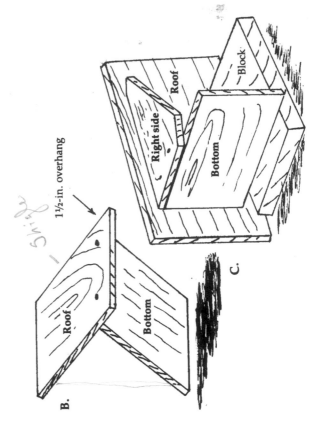

Note: Dimensions are in inches

B.

C.

Materials

Exterior plywood or cedar ⅝ in., 19½ by 17½ in.; or T 1-11 siding scraps:
Bottom—5¼ in. by 7½ in.
Sides (2)—each 10 by 5 in.
Back—9⅛ by 5¼ in.
Roof—9½ by 7¼ in.
Fourpenny galvanized box nails
Screws (2),1 in. long
Pieces of bark, or paint or stain to match the tree trunk
Brads, ½ to ¾ in.
Caulking compound

Tools

Square
Ruler
Plane
Rasp
Screwdriver
Brace, with 1½-in. expansion bit and ⅜-in. bit
Pencil
Saw
Hammer
Drill, with assorted small bits

Instructions

A. 1. With the square, outline all the parts on the weather surface of the material, according to the dimensions shown.

2. For the sides, mark 2 rectangles, each 10 by 5 in. Saw them out. Midway down the 10-in. dimension, run a line across at 90 degrees. Draw 2 more horizontal lines—1¼ in. down from the top and 1¼ in. up from the bottom—across at 90 degrees. Now, draw a line from the end of the midway mark at the edge, diagonally to the top and bottom corners. Saw along on the marks to achieve the shape shown in the drawing.

3. Saw out the other pieces, plane off the splinters, mark the pieces, and lay them aside.

B. 1. Nail the roof and bottom together, leaving a 1½-in. overhang for

D.

the roof. Be sure the roof extends 1 in. beyond each side of the bottom panel.

C. 1. Lay the unit on its left side with a block underneath so the roof hangs over the edge. Put 2 nails in the right side panel and nail it flush with the bottom. Put 1 nail into the side panel, through the roof.

D. 1. Now take the left side panel, measure 5¼ in. up from the bottom edge, and run a line across at 90 degrees. Center the hole along this line. Use an expansion bit to drill the entrance—1¼ in. for nuthatches and titmice, 1⅛ in. for chickadees. Smooth the edges with a rasp.

2. Turn the house over on its right side, as shown in the drawing. Put 2 nails on the entry (left side) panel to connect with the edge of the bottom panel. Position the entry panel, then drive the nails in just enough to hold. (You will later replace them with screws so the panel will be removable.)

3. Bevel the back panel ½ in. so the top and bottom edges slant forward. Try it for fit with the other pieces. About a ½-in. trian-

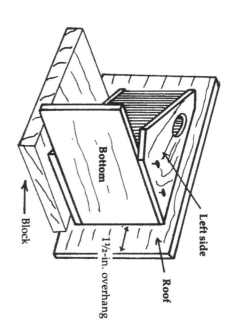

Bottom — Left side — Roof — 1½-in. overhang — Block

E.

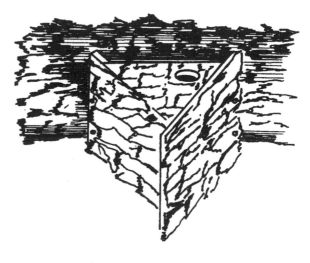

gular vent space should be at the top, and the panel should slip flush between the back edges of the 2 sides. Trim a bit more off the bevel if the sides and back are not flush and the back panel extends beyond the edges of the sides. Run a strip of caulking compound along the top, beveled edge of the back panel.

4. Nail the sides to the back panel, 2 nails in the permanent side, 1 temporary nail in the entrance panel. The slant roof should overhang the back about ¾ in. at the top.

5. If everything appears to be aligned, set 2 nails near the top of the roof to connect through the bevel in back. If the nails come through the back, bend them over. Now, put 2 nails into the bottom, angled to go directly through the bevel. Drive them in.

6. Drive 2 small holes, 1 on each side of the entry panel to connect with the edges of the back piece and the bottom. Countersink 2 screws, 1 in. long. Remove the temporary nails, using a block under the hammer to avoid tearing off the side.

7. Drill 2 holes, ⅜ in. in diameter, into the back piece, just above where the bevel edge joins the bottom panel. These holes will allow drainage during wet weather.

Bark roof

Inside curve

Note: Dimensions are in inches

Shelf

Bracket

A.

E. 1. Cover the unit with chunks of bark, fitted together. The house exterior does not need to be stylish, just disguised. Nail the bark on with brads that are long enough to go through the bark, but not so long that they will come through inside. Bark is unnecessary on the back since it will be against the tree. Sometimes it helps to have a sizable chunk of bark, through which you can drill an entrance hole. You can then fit it over the entry in the birdhouse, making it a more authentic nesting site.

2. If bark is difficult to find and the nesting season is months away, you can camouflage the house by mottling the exterior with paint or stain that blends with the tree trunk. If you must use paint or stain, however, be sure to let the coating age on the house for at least 2 weeks to prevent harming the birds.

3. To nail the unit to a tree trunk, put 2 nails in the top edge of the roof and 1 in the edge at the bottom. Leave the nails extending enough to be pulled so you can change its locations more easily. For chickadees and titmice, mount the house 6 to 15 ft. above the ground; for nuthatches, 12 to 20 ft.

Brown Creeper Cranny

Not really a birdhouse at all, this simple shelf and bark roof structure is purely an experimental attempt to coax the shy creeper into building its nest nearby. Made of only three pieces, it won't take much time to put together several, and your efforts may be rewarded by having tenant move in—if you live in their territory, that is.

Materials
Roof—bark, 12 by 8 in.
Shelf—straight-grained wood, 1 by 6 by 7 in.
Bracket—straight-grained wood, 2 by 4 by 6 in.
Sixpenny galvanized nails (4)
Tenpenny galvanized nails (2) or sixteen-penny nails (2)

Tools
Square   Pencil
Ruler   Saw
Plane   Keyhole saw
Hammer

Instructions

A. 1. Using the square and a pencil, mark out the parts in the dimensions shown. Saw them out and plane the edges. The outer edge of the shelf can be curved to fit the piece of bark. For the inside edge, you'll have to estimate. Use a dishpan or something that approximates the tree size, centering the curve so that it fits 1 in. inside the shelf ends.

B. 1. Start 2 sixpenny nails into the shelf, spaced to nail into the top (2½-in.) dimension of the bracket.

2. Place the pointed end of the bracket against the wall. Center the shelf over the bracket, back edges flush, and nail together.

C. 1. Using the tenpenny nails, secure the bracket to a tree or old stump, as shown. Place it about 6 ft. above the ground.

2. If the bark on the tree is thick, use a longer nail—sixteen-penny. However, with smaller nails there is less danger of splitting the bracket.

D. 1. Set a sixpenny nail, centered, about ½ in. from the top of the bark roof and tack it to the tree so that it overlaps the edge of the shelf about ½ in.

B.

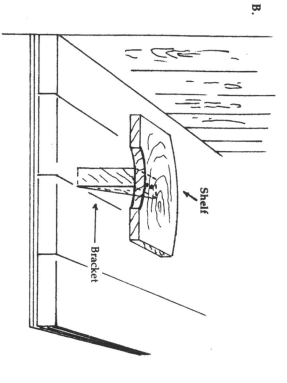

Shelf

Bracket

C.

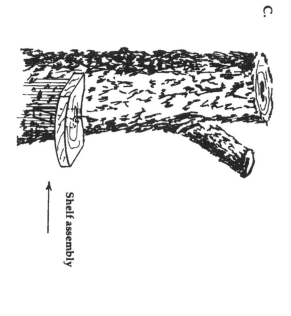

Shelf assembly

2. Now center another sixpenny nail near the bottom and tack it into the edge of the shelf. Hammer gently to avoid splitting the bark.

D.

Shelf assembly

Roof

Suggestions

Here are just a few things to keep in mind about placing bird-houses for tiny tenants.

1. Put houses up on tree trunks that have no limbs nearby.

2. Try several houses at different spots and different heights. Leave the nails extending slightly so that you can change locations easily.

3. Even though the openings to these houses are quite small, house sparrows have been known to slip through and take up residence, so watch carefully. (See the chapter about predators if this problem arises.)

4. Occasionally you may find that something has chiseled around the entrance as if trying to enlarge it. Take down the birdhouse and slightly enlarge the entrance with a rasp.

5. Since some of these birds like to enlarge their own nest cavities, try puffing wood chips in the bottom of the box. This may enhance its acceptability, especially for the red-breasted nuthatch.

Woodpecker Boxes

Northern flickers face stiff competition for cavities from European starlings.

Woodpeckers are noisy. Perhaps that is why some people might not want them around. In the breeding season, the males make a terrible racket, drumming on snags, telephone poles, downspouts, or even television antennas to signal each other or warn competitors.

But there are good reasons for having them close by. First, they are interesting to watch. Good parents, the male and female take turns excavating the nest cavity and feeding the young. With chisel-like bills and long, barbed tongues, they are admirably equipped to probe beneath the wood of old trees and dead snags for ants, beetles, and grubs that other birds cannot reach. Perhaps their greatest contribution is the nest holes they create anew each year, leaving a wide variety of nest sites for other species. Without woodpeckers, the survival of other hole nesters would be next to impossible.

Twenty-two species of woodpeckers, ranging in length from six to seventeen inches, are found in the United States and Canada. About half of these can be coaxed into using human-made nesting boxes. They include the northern flicker, the golden-fronted, red-headed, hairy, and downy woodpeckers.

Habits of the **northern flicker's** two forms, the red-shafted and the yellow-shafted (so-named for the color of the shafts on their primary wing feathers) are so similar that the two birds are considered as one species. They hybridize in a large overlap zone. Large birds, around 11 inches long, they both wear a black, crescent-shaped "sweater mark" across the chest. Their white rump patch helps in identification, as does their undulating flight.

The **"yellow-shafted" northern flicker** has bright yellow under the tail and underwing surfaces. It ranges east of the Rockies as far north as central Alaska to Newfoundland, and south through Texas, Florida, and even Cuba. Some winter in Arizona and California.

The **"red-shafted" northern flicker** is salmon-colored under the wings and tail. It ranges from southeast Alaska and central-North Dakota into northern Nicaragua and throughout the western United States. Northern flickers remain all winter on the Pacific slope. In northern sections of the East, they migrate south in the fall.

The red-shafted form favors farms and cutover lands, but is often found where fir trees still grow in the residential districts of large cities. The yellow-shafted form is a bird of the open countryside where hardwoods offer nesting sites. Both species are great ant-eaters and are often seen feeding on the ground in open fields, parks, and even yards. They frequent feeding stations when attracted by offerings of suet, fruit, and peanuts.

The northern flicker's nest cavity may contain five to 10 eggs. The incubation period lasts about two weeks and is a team effort. Both parents pipe food down clamoring throats until the young are ready to fly.

The **golden-fronted woodpecker**, which sports a gold spot on the back of its neck, is limited in range to Texas, southwest Oklahoma, and south to Nicaragua. About nine inches long, it feeds on ants, beetles, and larvae. It lays four to seven eggs in nest cavities, usually in April. Oak posts and live mesquite are its traditional sites for excavating nest cavities.

The **red-headed woodpecker** is about eight inches long and is distinguished from other species by a scarlet hood that extends down to its neck. This noisy bird is full of harsh scolding in summer, and feeds on insects and fruit. Its nest contains four to five eggs, and the parents often raise two broods per year.

The summer range of the red-headed woodpecker is from

New Brunswick, southern Quebec, southern Ontario, southern Manitoba, and southeast Alberta, south to Florida and the Gulf Coast; and west to central New Mexico, central Colorado, and eastern Wyoming. In winter, those north of Pennsylvania, West Virginia, Tennessee, and Oklahoma head south.

Essentially a forest dweller, the **hairy woodpecker** ranges from Newfoundland, Ontario, northern Manitoba, and southern Alaska, south to the Bahamas and Panama. Using an extraordinarily long, barbed tongue, it is a specialist in extracting the larvae of boring beetles from tunnels deep in the wood. Small as woodpeckers go—only about seven inches long— this bird cuts nest cavities in living or dead trees and deposits four white eggs. Only one brood is raised.

The six-inch **downy woodpecker** is a small edition of the hairy woodpecker. It, too, excavates a nest cavity in which four to five white eggs are laid. Its most important food is wood-boring ants, but it also likes caterpillars and weevils. Much of its feeding is done under the bark on outer, dead branches, in company with flocks of chickadees, nuthatches, and other birds. Its range includes Newfoundland, Ontario, southern Manitoba, southwest Mackenzie, and northwest Alaska, south to Florida, and the Gulf Coast, south-central Texas, southern New Mexico, and southern California.

Woodpecker Boxes

Each of the boxes described here is a simple, slant-roof design, so the building instructions are the same for all three boxes. The drawings give the specific dimensions for each one.

Materials—Flicker Box

Cedar boards or exterior plywood, ⅝ in., 39 by 24½ in.:
- Bottom—7 by 7 in.
- Sides (2)—each 19¾ by 18¾ by 7 in.
- Back—22 by 8¼ in.
- Front—19 by 8¼ in.
- Roof—10¼ by 10¼ in.

Fourpenny galvanized box nails
Sixpenny galvanized box nails (2)
Galvanized nail or right-angle screw hook, about 1½ in. long
Caulking compound
Sixteen-penny galvanized nail
Post (optional)—4 by 4 in. or 4 by 6 in., 9 ft. long or galvanized metal pole
Strapping brackets for mounting box
Predator baffle (pole- or post-mounted)

Materials—Golden-fronted, Red-headed, and Hairy Woodpecker Box

Cedar boards or exterior plywood, ⅝ in., 36¼ by 17¼ in.:
- Bottom—6 by 6 in.
- Sides (2)—each 14¾ by 13¾ by 6 in.
- Back—17 by 7¼ in.
- Front—14 by 7¼ in.
- Roof—9¼ by 9¼ in.

Fourpenny galvanized box nails
Sixpenny galvanized box nails (2)
Galvanized nail or right-angle screw hook, about 1½ in. long
Caulking compound
Sixteen-penny galvanized nail
Post (optional)— 4 by 4 in. or 4 by 6 in., 14 ft. long galvanized metal pole
Strapping brackets for mounting box
Predator baffle (pole- or post-mounted)

Materials—Downy Woodpecker Box

Cedar boards, or exterior plywood, ⅝ in., 25½ by 12¼ in.:
- Bottom—4 by 4 in.
- Sides (2)—each 9¾ by 9 by 4 in.
- Back—12 by 5¼ in.
- Front—9¼ by 5¼ in.
- Roof—6½ by 6½ in.

Fourpenny galvanized box nails
Sixpenny galvanized box nails (2)
Galvanized nail or right-angle screw hook, about 1½ in. long
Caulking compound
Sixteen-penny galvanized nail
Post (optional)—4 by 4 in. or 4 by 6 in., 9 ft. long or galvanized metal pole
Strapping brackets for mounting box
Predator baffle (pole- or post-mounted)

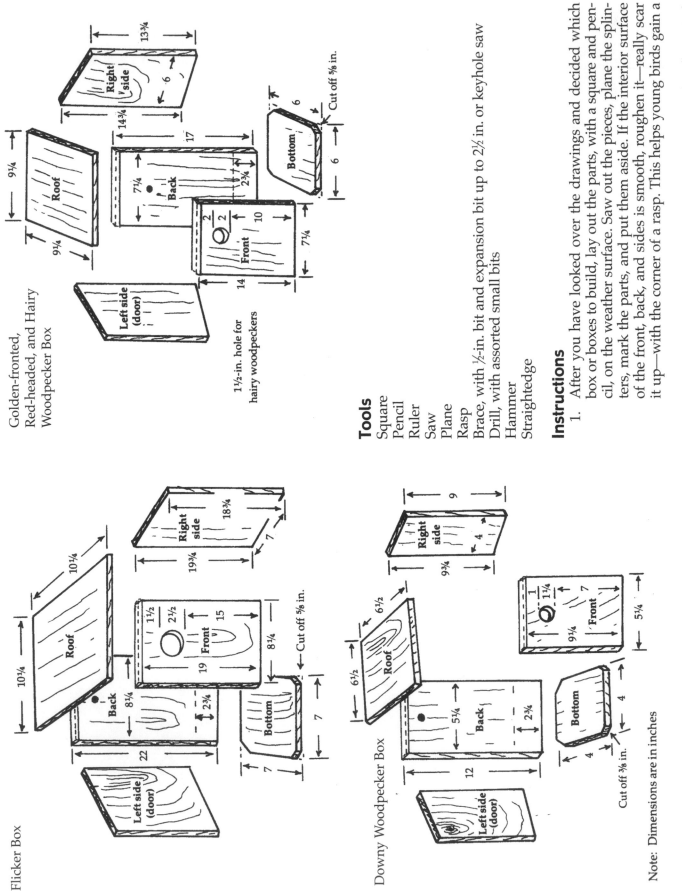

Golden-fronted,
Red-headed, and Hairy
Woodpecker Box

13¾

Right side

6

9¾

Roof

9¼

9¼

14¾

17

7¼

Back

2¾

Front

2

2

10

7¼

14

Left side
(door)

Bottom

6

6

Cut off ⅝ in.

1½-in. hole for
hairy woodpeckers

Tools

Square
Pencil
Ruler
Saw
Plane
Rasp
Brace, with ½-in. bit and expansion bit up to 2½ in. or keyhole saw
Drill, with assorted small bits
Hammer
Straightedge

Instructions

1. After you have looked over the drawings and decided which box or boxes to build, lay out the parts, with a square and pencil, on the weather surface. Saw out the pieces, plane the splinters, mark the parts, and put them aside. If the interior surface of the front, back, and sides is smooth, roughen it—really scar it up—with the corner of a rasp. This helps young birds gain a

Flicker Box

18¾

Right
side

7

19¾

10¼

Roof

10¼

1½

2½

15

Front

19

8¼

Cut off ⅝ in.

Back

8¼

2¾

Bottom

7

7

7

22

Left side
(door)

Downy Woodpecker Box

9

Right
side

4

9¾

6½

Roof

6½

6½

1

1¼

7

Front

9¼

5¼

5¼

Back

2¾

Bottom

4

12

4

4

Cut off ⅜ in.

Left side
(door)

Note: Dimensions are in inches

foothold when trying to climb to the hole when exiting the box. Cut back the corners of the bottom piece.

2. In the back panel, drill a ½-in. hole 2 in. down from the top and centered horizontally. (On the downy woodpecker box, center the hole 1 in. down.) Bevel the back ⅛ in. toward the interior surface. On the front panel, bevel ⅛ in. toward the weather surface.

3. Drill the entrance as shown for each box, using a keyhole saw or expansion bit on the larger boxes. If you have neither, then draw the circle and drill a series of ½- to 1-in. holes just inside the circumference. Chew out the hole with a rasp, rounding the edges. Woodpeckers won't mind a few irregularities.

4. Draw a line across the interior surface of the back, 2¾ in. up from the bottom. Extend it across the edges and the weather surface.

5. Next, draw a line across the interior surface of the front panel, 1 in. up from the bottom, and extend it over both edges.

6. Draw 1 more line across the interior surface of the right side panel, 1 in. up from the bottom, and extend it across the edges.

7. To begin assembly, start 2 nails on the weather surface of the right side panel to come out ¼ in. *below* the line. Do not get the nails too close to the edges of the side panel, because the bottom edge, to which you will nail the side panel, has the corners cut off. Place the "decornered" bottom on edge, against a wall. Lay the side panel across, with the line matching the interior surface of the bottom. The wall will keep the 2 pieces flush. Drive the nails part way in.

8. Place the unit on its side edge and lay the back panel on, flush with the side piece. Match the lines. Put 2 nails through the back, part way into the edge of the side panel. The top of the side panel should be ¼ to ⅜ in. below the back. Bring the outer corner of the bottom into position. Drive the nails part way in. Put another nail into the bottom, near the inner corner. If everything lines up, drive in all the nails.

9. Turn the unit on its back and lay the front piece on, flush with the side. Match the lines. Drive 2 nails through the front, part way into the edge of the side. Check the bottom for alignment. Pull it into position, hold, and drive a nail part way in the outer corner. Put 1 more nail into the inner corner. Check the side

Woodpecker Box Mounts

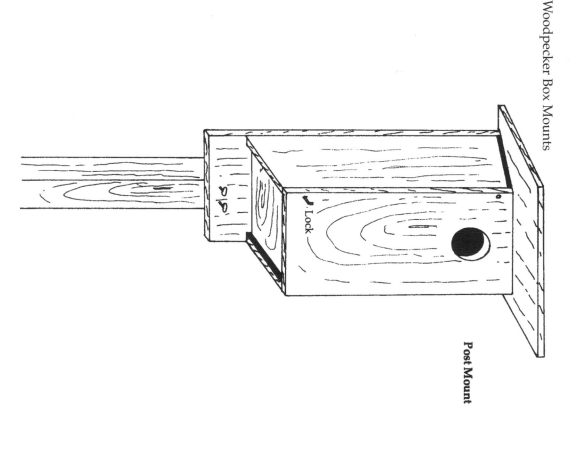

Post Mount

and front panel. There should be a ⅜-in. drop below the bottom to allow for rain drip.

10. Lay a straightedge across the front and back panels. There should be a ¼ to ⅜-in. gap between the top of the side and the straightedge. If it all fits, drive in all the nails.

11. Slip the left side panel, which will be the door, into place and check it for fit, lightly shaving off the edges with a sharp plane if the fit is too tight.

12. Mark 1 in. down from the top of the front panel near the edge. Draw a line at 90 degrees from this point, across the left side panel. Following the line, drive a sixpenny nail through the front panel and part way into the edge of the side panel. Repeat through the back panel. Before driving the nails all the way in, test the door hinge by pulling from the bottom.

13. Tack the door shut and drill a small hole into the edge, through the front panel near the bottom. Slip in a lock nail or use a right-angle screw hook to hold it shut. Remove the temporary nail.

14. Now for the roof. Run a strip of caulking compound along the beveled edge on the back panel. Set the box upright, using a block under the front edge. Start 2 nails in the rear portion of the roof, to connect with the top edge of the back panel. Place the roof in position, flush with the back and with an equal overhang on both sides. Drive the nails part way in. Line up 2 more nails to connect with the top edge of the front panel. Drive them part way in. Check it over, then drive in all the nails. Do not put any nails through the roof, into the sides.

15. To mount the box on a post or snag, drive a sixteen-penny galvanized nail at an angle in the desired location. For flickers and downies, the box should be 6 to 20 ft. above the ground; for red-headed, golden-fronted, and hairy woodpeckers, 12 to 20 ft. above the ground. Hook the box through the ½-in. hole in the back. Put 2 more nails into the edge, where the back panel extends below the bottom. Do not drive the nails all the way, in case you want to change locations later on. *Remember to use*

Snag Mount

The Original Birdhouse Book

a predator-proof baffle mounted below the box in areas where nest box predators are prevalent.

Suggestions

Many times woodpeckers will pass up what seems to be a perfectly suitable box in order to excavate their own nest cavities. Here are a few suggestions that might help to improve your success.

1. For larger birds such as flickers and golden-fronted woodpeckers, mount the box in the sun where it can be seen easily. For hairy woodpeckers and downies, be sure the tree trunk site is free of nearby limbs.

2. Be sure the box is high enough for each species, as indicated in the instructions. Put a predator guard on the post (see "Predators and Competitors" starting on page 72).

3. Woodpeckers, particularly flickers, generally have a strong desire to get in and dig. It's an important part of their courtship and breeding cycle. Give them something to do by filling the nest box, floor to ceiling, with tightly packed wood chips (sawdust works, too, in areas that receive little rain. In wet areas, sawdust soaks up and retains moisture, which can hinder development of eggs and young birds). After they toss out all the material, add another four inches.

4. If there are no takers, tack some bark on the outside of the box so it blends with nearby tree trunks. This may help to satisfy house-hunting woodpeckers.

5. Once you know from your visits that the woodpeckers are on eggs or that the eggs have hatched, resist the urge to peek into the nest. Nestling woodpeckers older than 12 days from hatching are excitable and may attempt flight before they are ready.

6. Flickers will sometimes attack a house, particularly one with shake siding. Try a flicker box over the area they are pecking. The box will also have a hollow sound when pecked, which may have been what attracted them to the shakes.

7. For the different species of woodpeckers that live in your neighborhood, build a number of boxes and place them in several locations. The woodpeckers will decide which is best. And you never know—other desirable birds may be attracted.

Wood Duck Boxes

Young wood ducks leap from the nest box to the ground when they fledge. Their light weight allows them to float to a gentle landing.

Not everyone is fortunate enough to live near water—a pond or small stream or marsh area—frequented by wood ducks. But if you live in such an area, think about putting up wood duck boxes. When placed in proper locations, wood duck boxes are readily accepted by these small birds, which weigh only 1½ pounds. Your efforts will be rewarded—wood ducks are delightful to have around. Few birds are as colorful as the male and the birds' antics will keep you at the window for long periods, particularly if you scatter a little feed within watching distance.

Wood ducks have had their ups and downs. Plentiful before the 1880s, they then fell into steady decline and by 1900 were faced with possible extinction. Due to concerted conservation efforts during the last 100 years, their numbers have increased. Today an estimated 2.5 to 3.5 million wood ducks live in North America, ranging throughout the Mississippi basin to the eastern seaboard, north into parts of Canada, and south to Florida. A smaller population is found along the Pacific slope from California to southern British Columbia.

In early spring, the female leaves for the nesting site. The male with whom she mated in late fall or winter just tags along. Her sense of location is highly accurate—she will always return to the area in which she was hatched, sometimes even to the same nest box. The male might have originated in an area 200 miles away.

Shallow water zones (around 18 inches deep), with islands, grass, exposed snags, and protective cover are ideal nesting sites. Swamp areas with old snags or even ponds bordered by hardwoods appear to be favorites. Often the pair will fly up and down small streams, looking from side to side for a nest cavity that is large enough. (During this search, curious wood ducks have been known to tumble down chimneys of vacant summer cabins, and eventually die of starvation. Screening chimney openings prevents this.)

Since the wood ducks bring no material into the nest except down plucked from the female's feathers, it is important to have debris at the bottom of the nesting cavity. One egg a day is deposited until there are 10 to 15. A 30-day incubation period begins immediately thereafter. During this time, the female leaves the nest in the morning and again in the late afternoon to feed. The length of time she spends away from the nest depends on the outside temperature. While she is gone, eggs are tucked cozily beneath layers of down.

Two or three days before hatching, the youngsters begin making sounds inside the shell. The mother talks back with low clucks, which seems to establish the maternal bond. About 24 hours after hatching, she moves outside and begins calling to the nestlings. Looking like popcorn, as they hop about excitedly, the ducklings hitch their way, one by one, to the nestbox entrance and fling themselves into space. After falling like tiny powder puffs 30 feet or more to hit the ground, they bounce softly and then run to join their mother. She may lead them as much as a mile overland to the desired body of water for rearing.

Meanwhile, the male has drifted off with the fellows, and will soon begin to molt into a neutral color. For about two weeks he will hide out until he can fly again. By October, with new plumage, he will head south, meet another female, and follow wherever she leads him the next spring.

Raising a brood of wood ducks is a monumental task. Only about 40 to 50 percent of them reach maturity. From the air they are preyed on by hawks and owls. In the south, cottonmouth moccasins strike them down. Raccoon, mink, or even large bullfrogs take their toll. Snapping turtles, bass, pickerel, and northern pike snatch the ducklings from beneath the surface. Adult birds are not safe either. Occasionally they will blunder into traps set for muskrat and mink, or be taken by other predators, or duck hunters.

It is questionable whether the present number of wood ducks can be maintained. Loss of wooded wetlands to development and agriculture continues at a fast pace, reducing the wood duck's preferred nesting habitat. You can help the wood duck population by providing nesting boxes. There are never enough.

Wood Duck Box

This is the largest bird box you will be building, using the plans in this book. Before starting, be sure that your supply of scraps contains pieces large enough to accommodate the required dimensions. And don't forget the four inches of wood chips in the bottom. It's a very important cushion for the eggs.

Materials

Cedar, pine, or exterior plywood, ⅝ in., 55 by 37¼ in.; or T 1-11 siding scraps:

- Bottom—10½ by 10½ in.
- Sides (2)—each 27¾ by 27 by 10½ in.
- Back—31 by 113h in.
- Front—27 by 113h in.
- Roof—14 by 14 in.

Fourpenny galvanized box nails
Galvanized hardware cloth, ¼-in. mesh, 4 by 19 in.
Staples, #5, wire brad
Cleats (2)—board, 1 by 4 by 10¼ in., ripped in half to make each cleat 1 by 1¾ by 10¼ in.
Screen door hooks and eyes (2 pairs)
Sixteen-penny galvanized framing nails (2)
Galvanized pipe, 1½ in.; long enough to extend 4 ft. above water
Threaded pipe flange
Flathead screws (3), #8, ¾ in. long
Strap iron, 2 pieces, each 30 in. long, 3¾ in. wide, ⅛ to $^{3}/_{16}$ in. thick
Metal hose clamp, ¼ in. in diameter
Wood chips, enough to fill space that is 4 by 10½ by 10½ in.

Tools

Square	Pencil
Ruler	Saw
Rasp	Plane
Compass, or 3-in. jar lid	Hammer
Screwdriver	

Brace, with 3-in. expansion bit, or ⅝-in. bit and keyhole saw

Instructions

A. 1. Check over the dimensions. With a square and pencil, lay out all the parts on the weather surface, with grooves running down the sides and slope of the roof, not across. Then saw out all the pieces. Be sure the corners of the bottom are cut off, ⅝ in. back. Drill a ⅝-in. hole, centered in the back panel, 2 in. down from the top. Bevel the back and front panels ⅛ in. at the top to accommodate the roof slant.

2. On the front panel, center a 4- by 3-in. rectangle 2½ in. down from the top, as shown in the drawing, but remember that you beveled off ⅛ in. and allow for it. Use a compass or 3-in. jar lid to circumscribe a semicircle at each end of the rectangle. Use a 3-in. expansion bit to cut the ends of the rectangle. If you do not have an expansion bit, then drill a ⅝-in. hole just inside the curve and cut out the entrance with a keyhole saw to give the opening an elliptical shape. Round off the edges with a rasp.

3. Draw a line across the interior surface of the back panel, 3⅝ in. up from the bottom. Extend it over the edge and across the weather surface. (This is to match up with the outside surface of the bottom panel.) Next, draw a line across the interior surface of the right side panel, 1 in. up from the bottom. Extend it across the edges and the weather surface. Put 1 more line, 1 in. up from the bottom, across the interior surface of the front panel, and extend it across the edges and the weather surface.

4. Start the assembly by putting 2 nails in the right side panel, to come out ¼ in. below the line on the other side. Place the bottom on edge. Lay the side panel across with the line marked on it matching the interior surface of the bottom panel. Be sure the edges are flush by sliding the 2 pieces against a wall. Drive the nails part way in.

5. Turn the joined pieces on the side edge. Position the back, matching its line with the outside surface of the bottom and

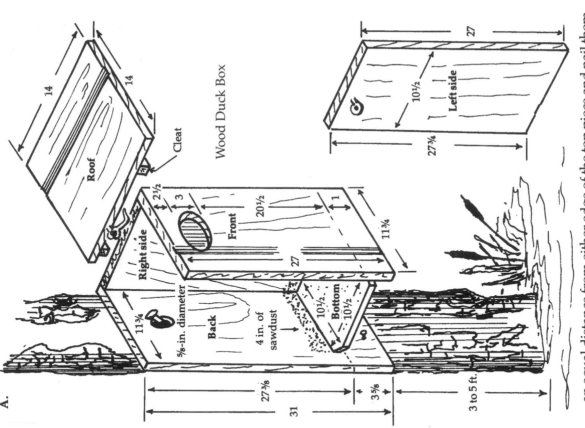

A.

Roof
14
14
Cleat

Wood Duck Box

Right side
Front
Back
2½
3
20½
1
27
11¾
11¾
⅝-in. diameter
4 in. of sawdust
10½
Bottom
10½
3⅝
27⅞
31
3 to 5 ft.

Left side
27
10½
27¾

an equal distance from either edge of the top piece and nail them just inside the lines. Clinch the nails if they come through.

12. Check the top for fit. Set screen door hooks and eyes on each side to hold it firm.

making its top flush with the side panel. Put 3 nails through the back, into the edge of the side. Drive the nails part way in. The back should extend 3⅝ in. below the bottom panel. The side should slope evenly, its top edge matching the top of the back and front panels. Hold the front panel in position and check it.

6. Put a nail through the back near the outer corner of the bottom, line it up, hold, and drive the nail part way in. Put another nail into the inside corner. Look over the alignment. If it is good, drive in all the nails.

7. You are now ready for the front, but first let's get the hardware cloth nailed on the inside so you won't have to crawl in and do it later. Tack a 4-in. width of hardware cloth, 19 in. long, from the edge of the entrance to within 1½ in. of the floor. You can tack the material flat using staples and a hammer (a staple gun is fine if you have one). Make sure you do not leave *any* rough ends or edges exposed that might scratch or cut the birds.

8. Position the front, the bottom of it even with the side panel. Put 3 nails through the front, part way into the edge of the side panel. Line up the bottom, hold, and put 1 nail through the front into the inside corner. Put 1 more nail into the inside corner, but keep in mind that the corners have been cut back—don't get your nails too close. Check the alignment, then drive in all the nails.

9. Slip the left side into place. Line it up and nail it—3 nails into the front panel, 3 into the back, and 2 along the bottom.

10. The roof on this house is removable so you can inspect the nest and clean out the box. Lay the top in position, the rear portion flush with the back. Slide it 2 or 3 in. to one side and mark the inside of the roof along the edges of the front and back panels. Draw lines across at these marks inside the roof, paralleling the front and back. These lines are used to line up the front and back cleats.

11. To make 2 cleats, take a 1 by 4-in. board, 10¼ in. long. Down the center, ripsaw 2 pieces, about 1¾ in. wide. Check the length inside the box. If the cleats are too long, shave the ends a bit. Place them

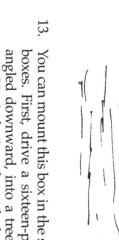

B.

Hook and eye

Threaded pipe flange

1½-in. pipe

4 ft.

13. You can mount this box in the same manner as other slant roof boxes. First, drive a sixteen-penny galvanized framing nail, angled downward, into a tree or snag. Leave 1½ in. sticking out. Hook the box through the hole in the back. Place 2 more

sixteen penny nails into the extension, beneath, but do not drive them all the way in. This is an advantage. With a small wrecking bar you can quickly pull the nails and relocate the box if necessary.

B. 1. You can place wood duck boxes in farm ponds by incorporating 1½-in. galvanized pipe, driven deep into the mud bottom, to extend 4 ft. above the surface of the water. Underneath the bottom of the box, center a threaded pipe flange and fasten it with screws. Rotate the box onto the pipe threads on top of the pipe.

2. Extra bracing may include 2 pieces of strap iron, fastened to the sides with screws. Angle them inward beneath, then secure them to the pipe with a metal hose clamp. Painting will hold off rusting. In snake country, leave them off.

Metal Wood Duck Box

The Metal Wood Duck Box, which rather resembles the Tin Woodman of *The Wizard of Oz*, is another approach to furnishing nesting sites for wood ducks. It has been used experimentally in the Midwest and South to deter raids by raccoons, and has been quite effective. The best predator-proofing is to mount the house on a galvanized metal pole with a pole-mounted predator baffle to prevent predator access. A coating of auto undercoat, roughened, provides the climbing ladder for young ducklings. Painting the box a light pastel (be sure to use an exterior latex brand) will help reflect the sun's rays and keep it cooler inside.

Materials

Galvanized furnace pipe, unassembled, 28 gauge, 48 in. long, 12 in. in diameter

Panhead metal screws (10), ¼ in. long, ⅛ in. in diameter

Flashing compound, 1 pint

Galvanized hardware cloth, ¼-in. mesh, 4 by 18 in.

Spray-on auto undercoat, 1 quart

Strap iron, 1 piece, 1¼ by ³⁄₁₆ by 75 in.

Strap iron, 1 piece, 1¼ by ³⁄₁₆ by 57 in.

Stove bolts (3), ¾ in. long, ³⁄₁₆ in. in diameter

Nuts and washers (3 pairs)

Cedar, or exterior plywood, ⅝ in., 12½ by 12½ in.

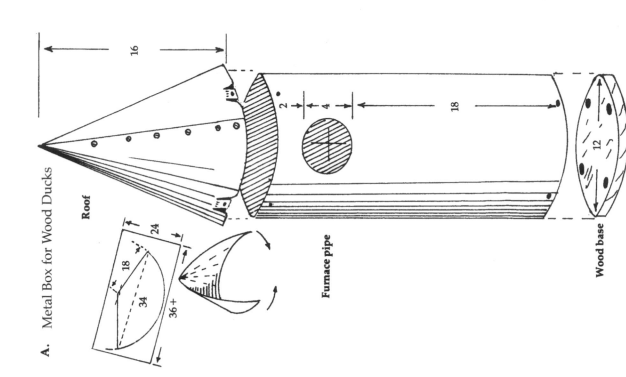

A. Metal Box for Wood Ducks

Fourpenny galvanized box nails (4)
Roundhead screws (4), ¾ in. long, 3⁄16 in. in diameter
Exterior latex paint, light pastel shade, 1 quart
Lag bolts (2), 2½ in. long, ¼ in. in diameter
Wood chips, enough to cover several inches inside the box

Tools

Yardstick	Pencil
Square	Tin snips
Compass	Metal file
String, 36 in. long	Hammer
Screwdriver	C clamps (2)
Razor blade	Putty knife
Pliers	Keyhole saw
Adjustable crescent wrench	Brace, with ½-in. wood bit
Paintbrush	Extension ladder or boat
Wood, 1 by 2 by 30 in. long	Sixpenny nails (2)
Large bolt or fishing sinker	

Scotch Brand Filament Tape, ½ in. wide, 36 in. long
Drill, and bits for metal—$3⁄8$ in., $9⁄64$ in., and $3⁄32$ in. in diameter

Instructions

A. 1. With the yardstick, measure 24 in. up on the furnace pipe at several points and mark with a pencil. This material will be curled, ready for assembly by interlocking the edges. Lay it flat, edges down. Lay the square across, press it with your foot, and draw a line connecting the marks you made. Cut along this line. Set one section aside for the roof.

2. Keeping the metal flat, place a mark at the top of 1 piece, 12 in. from an edge. Use the square to draw a vertical line 6 in. long. Place a cross mark 4 in. down from the top.

3. Set the compass on a 2-in. radius, place the point on the cross mark, and draw a 4-in. circle.

4. Put a board beneath and drill a ⅜-in. hole just inside the edge of the circle.

5. With tin snips, cut out the 4-in. entrance. File off any sharp snags.

6. Place the interlocking edges together and flex the metal to interconnect them, forming a tube. Set it aside.

The Original Birdhouse Book

7. To make the roof, spread the other half section, curled edges down, and center a mark within 1 in. of the top (the long edge). Hold your foot down to keep it as flat as possible.

8. Put a loop in the end of the string to hold the pencil. Measure down the string 18 in. Hold it with your thumbnail at that point on the center mark and swing the pencil along the 18-in. radius, making light dash marks on the metal in a half circle. Keep marking until you have a suitable line.

9. Lay the yardstick *below* the center mark, across the curve. Where it intersects at 34 in., make cross marks. Draw radius lines from the cross marks to the center point that you marked first. Lay the square ¼ in. below the center point, parallel to the top edge of the metal. Draw a mark across the 2 radius lines.

10. You now have a pattern that resembles a double portion of pie with a blunted end. Use the tin snips to cut along the radius lines, the curved bottom edge, and the blunt end. Turn the piece over.

11. During this step, because it is curved for pipe purposes, the metal will fight back as you try to form a cone. Flatten the metal as much as possible without creasing it.

12. Lay the long edge of the square near the 18-in. radius, ¼ in. from the edge at the top and 1 in. from the edge at the bottom. Draw a line. Step on the square with both feet to hold it down. Slip a screwdriver under the edge of the metal and pry upward gently, all along the edge, until it sets about ¼ in. off the floor near the bottom. Hammer along the edge until it is fairly even.

13. Move the square 3 in. in from the first mark at the bottom and about ¼ in. closer to the center at the top. Draw a line, set the square, plant both feet, slip the screwdriver underneath, and pry gently upward all the way along until it sets at about ½ in. to the other side and do the same—1 in., then 3 in. Continue at 3-in. intervals, first one side, then the other. As the metal curls, you will not be able to get the square over the edge at the top. Get it as close as you can, using the narrow edge of the square.

14. The cone shape will form, with creases along the radius lines,

---

converging at the top. Center the last crease. It will be about 3¾ in. from the other two. Lay the cone on a board. Place a 1 by 2-in. piece of wood over each crease and hammer it flat. Squeeze the cone edges together until the bottom overlaps at 1¼ in. Clamp the overlap. Press the top together until the edges overlap about ⅜ in. and the hole is nearly closed. Hold the overlap near the top with wraps of Scotch Brand Filament Tape.

15. Test the cone by placing it over the furnace pipe. It should extend about 1 to 1¼ in. below the top edge. Starting near the bottom, drill a series of 6 holes, ³⁄₃₂ in. in diameter and 3 in. apart, centered in the overlap. Don't worry about the Scotch tape. Drill right through and set the metal panhead screws so they are snug, but not tight enough to strip the threads. Unwrap the tape and cut it away with a razor blade. With a putty knife, press flashing compound into the seam along the edge, over the screws, and in any opening left in the top. Trim the irregularities off the bottom.

16. At 10¼-in. intervals, cut 4 tabs, 1 in. wide and ¾ in. deep, along the bottom. Round off all sharp corners. Fit the cone over the furnace pipe, level it, and tape it in place. Drill a ³⁄₃₂-in. hole through each tab, ¼ in. from the bottom and through the furnace pipe. Set the panhead screws snugly to fasten the top. Remove the tape.

17. Lengthwise, curl the ¼-in. mesh hardware cloth to lie flat inside the pipe. Make cuts along the top edge (4-in. dimension), ½ in. deep and ½ in. apart.

18. Fit the piece vertically inside, flat against the wall, and curl the tabs over the bottom edge of the entrance. Use pliers to clamp them.

19. Spray the auto undercoat over the hardware cloth, tacking it to the inside. Be sure that no stray wires are sticking up. Thoroughly spray around the edge of the entrance.

B. 1. Bend the two pieces of strap iron as shown in the drawing. Use the square to check the angles. Clamp the upper section together. Measure, mark, and drill ¼-in. holes. Separate them.

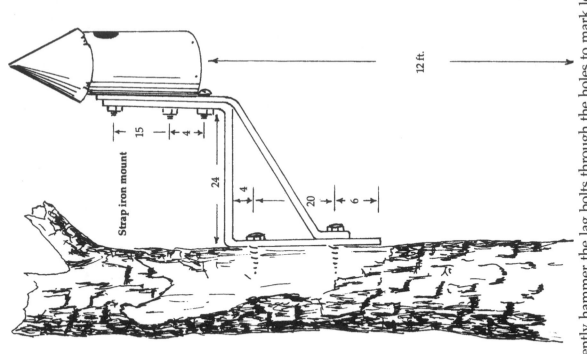

B.

Strap iron mount — 15, 4, 4, 24, 4, 20, 6 — 12 ft.

Drill a ⅜-in. hole 4 in. below the horizontal extender. Clamp both pieces together again and drill a ⅜-in. hole where the two pieces connect near the bottom.

2. Draw a vertical line down the back side of the furnace pipe. Center the clamped assembly on the line and mark the two upper holes. Drill these into the pipe using a ¼-in. bit. Slip the stove bolts, nuts, and washers in place and fasten the pipe tightly to the bracket.

3. With the compass, draw a circle 12 in. in diameter on the ⅝-in. plywood. Cut it out with a keyhole saw. Drill four to six ½-in. holes equally spaced near the perimeter for drainage.

4. Slip the circle of wood into the open end of the pipe (see drawing A), leaving a ⅛-in. margin of metal below. Tack in four places around the circumference, about 9¾ in. apart. Pull out one nail at a time, drill a ³⁄₁₆-in. hole, ¼ in. deep but no more. Ream the metal to make the hole slightly larger and set the screw so it is snug, but not too tight.

5. Give the box assembly and bracket 2 coats of paint.

6. When a boat is used to install the box on a snag surrounded by water, the lower end of the mounting bracket needs to be only 5 or 6 ft. up—a comfortable working range. On land, the lower end of the bracket ought to be 10 ft. or more above the ground (to prevent curious youngsters from disturbing the nesting wood duck). For this you will need an extension ladder. Take along a 1 by 2-in. piece of wood, 30 in. long, with two ⅜-in. holes drilled to match those in the bracket. You will need a 36-in. piece of string, with a heavy bolt or sinker tied to one end, plus a hammer, 2 sixpenny nails, and a crescent wrench. Don't forget to bring along a plastic bag of wood chips, enough to fill several inches in the bottom of the box.

7. Pick a snag. Be sure that the wood is sound. Plant the ladder securely, climb up, end tack the top of the 1 by 2 on the trunk. Hang the string with the weight on the end and adjust the 1 by 2 so that it is vertical. Tack the lower end.

8. Gently hammer the lag bolts through the holes to mark locations. Twist them out, drop the 1 by 2, and hammer the bolts into the snag about 1 in. to enlarge the holes. Twist them out with the crescent wrench.

The Original Birdhouse Book

9. Bring up the box and bracket assembly. This is awkward, so watch your step, particularly with the added weight of wood chips in the box.

10. Set the bracket in position, resting it on your shoulder, and hammer in the top bolt until it seems firm. Now, hammer in the lower bolt until it holds, then twist it in farther. Continue with the wrench, twisting on the top bolt until it is tight, then the lower one.

11. This type of box is not easily opened, so leave it—except for annual cleanout. This can be done by removing the 4 bottom screws. You will need to set the extension ladder against the snag at a fairly shallow slant in order to work beneath the box comfortably.

12. To check this style of box during the nesting season, affix a small mirror to the end of an extendable pole. Have a partner hold the pole so the mirror reflects the inside of the box while you focus your binoculars on the mirror's image.

Suggestions

Here are a few reminders to give you and the wood duck a better chance.

1. Take your time. First examine the habitat to be sure wood ducks frequent the area. Then build only two or three boxes—wood duck boxes are super sized, and you can always build more next season.

2. Be sure to install a four-inch width of hardware cloth (¼-inch mesh, galvanized) from the floor to the entrance. Even if the interior wall appears to be rough, the galvanized mesh will ensure extra grip for tiny toenails. This point cannot be over-stressed. The climbing ladder is essential for young ducklings to make their escape. Otherwise they might remain in the nest and perish. Take care to leave no sharp points or wire edges that may cause injury.

3. Add four inches of wood chips to the bottom of the box and keep it fresh from one year to the next. This is something the ducks look for when selecting a nest, and is essential during the incubation period.

4. The box should be tight along the seams. Wood ducks appreciate darkness inside. And ventilation is not so critical as it is with small birds that remain in the nest for weeks, because young wood ducks leave the box about twenty-four hours after hatching. Incubation occurs early enough to avoid most of the hot weather—in case you're worried about the mother's comfort.

5. If you mount the box on a tree, be sure to place the box near or over water and in a place where heavy foliage will not hide the location. Boxes on lone snags, away from trees, seem to be the most acceptable human-made nesting sites for these ducks. The boxes, once mounted, should be tipped forward so rain cannot run into the entrance.

6. Boxes can be about 50 feet apart. Wood ducks mind their own business and do not seem to battle over territory the way smaller birds do.

7. In addition to having your boxes in the open, it doesn't hurt to paint them light pastel colors to heighten visibility. (Use an exterior latex house paint.) Some evidence suggests they are then more readily accepted. Although having boxes that stand out on open lands frequented by strangers could invite vandalism, painted boxes are a good idea in areas where someone can watch them.

8. Check the condition of the boxes in January or early February. Unplug the drain holes, throw out the egg shells, change the wood chips bedding, and destroy the bee and wasp nests. (Wood ducks don't like bees and wasps.) Also throw out old starling nests. If you find a screech-owl, kestrel, squirrel, hooded merganser, or perhaps a goldeneye inside the box, leave it alone—and head for the shop to build another box!

whistle, descending rapidly in a series of bounces. Listen! You may hear it outside at night.

There are three species of screech-owls that live in North America—the **eastern screech-owl**, the **western screech-owl**, and the **whiskered screech-owl**. Two of the three, the eastern and western screech-owls are widely distributed throughout the continent. Eastern screeches are found from the Great Plains, eastward. Western screeches are found from the Rocky Mountains, westward, and as far north as southern Alaska. The whiskered screech-owl's range is limited to a small portion of southeastern Arizona, so we'll concentrate on the two more widespread species for this book.

Both western and eastern screech-owls can be identified by their red, brown, or gray color, barred feathers of a darker shade, and ear tufts. Screech-owls are about eight to 10 inches long. Feeding mainly on rodents and occasionally small birds such as house sparrows, they may hunt along roadways, sometimes colliding with automobiles as they swoop low in the blinding headlights. Screech-owls inhabit old orchards with open fields nearby or open areas bordered by hardwoods.

Screech-owls are attracted to abandoned woodpecker holes for nesting accommodations. Often they will select properly placed human-made boxes, where they will lay five to eight white eggs.

Perhaps the oddest looking bird you will ever encounter is the common **barn owl**, which has an all-white, monkey face bordered in a cinnamon color. Its back and wings are buff, mottled with gray. Its underparts, lightly speckled with brown, may be cinnamon-colored or white. From 15 to 20 inches long, it has a wingspan of about 45 inches.

The barn owl roosts in open barns or vacated buildings in open country, and nests in church steeples, building cornices, old shed, wells or abandoned warehouses. It may nest in human-made boxes that have little nest material. Eggs number five to 10, and are laid over a two-week period. Incubation begins after the first is laid, so the hatchlings are often varied in size—a stair-step series from the smallest to the largest.

Rodents, often those that do the most damage to farm crops, are this bird's principle food. Barn owls are generally found throughout the United States, southern Canada, and Mexico. In northern climates, many migrate south.

The **American kestrel** or "sparrow hawk" is a falcon that preys largely on grasshoppers and large insects. Sometimes it will

Screech-owls often peer out of a cavity or nest box to soak up the sun's warmth.

Owl & Kestrel Boxes

Owls and kestrels are effective hunters of mice, rats, other small mammals, and large insects. Some people are squeamish about avian predators, but they play an important role in our ecosystems, even when they occasionally prey upon other birds.

Certain species of owls regularly nest in cavities. So do kestrels, commonly referred to as "sparrow hawks." Both, under the right circumstances, will nest in human-made boxes.

You may not have noticed, but it is possible that owls live in your neighborhood, particularly if your residence is near broad fields bordered by timber. Occasionally you may see one in the car headlights at night, or hear its call. Owls down their prey whole. Their digestive juices dissolve the prey and the undigestibles are regurgitated as fur pellets later. These can be a telltale sign, indicating that you live in owl country. Be especially alert for fur pellets beneath outbuildings or trees.

One of the owls you may attract to a nesting box is the **screech-owl**, which doesn't really screech at all. Its call is more of a capture small rodents. This handsome bird may often be seen perched on telephone wires or posts near open fields along the outskirts of cities. Eight to 10 inches long and generally reddish in color with a black moustache mark and brown or bluish wings, it can often be seen hovering over open fields, fluttering to hold its position as it searches for movement below.

Common throughout North America, the little kestrel is partial to large abandoned woodpecker holes. It may occasionally accept human-made nest boxes, where it lays four to six eggs. While its main diet consists of insects and rodents, it has been known to kill small birds, but this is rare.

Screech-owl and Kestrel Box

This simple box will work for screech-owls as well as kestrels so long as you do not put it up in the same kind of location. The procedure for building it is much the same as that used for the wood duck box except that this house has a hinge-nail side opening instead of a removable top.

Materials

Cedar boards or exterior plywood, ⅝ in., 45 by 27¼ in.; or T 1-11 siding scraps:

Bottom—8 by 8 in.
Sides (2)—each 15¾ by 14¾ by 8 in.
Back—19 by 9¼ in.
Front—15 by 9¼ in.
Roof—11¼ by 11¼ in.

Fourpenny galvanized box nails
Galvanized nail or right-angle screw hook, either one about 1½ in. long
Caulking compound
Sixteen-penny galvanized framing nail
Galvanized siding nails (2)

Tools

Square
Ruler
Plane
Hammer
Brace, with 3-in. expansion bit, or keyhole saw, and ½-in. bit

Pencil
Saw
Rasp

A.

Screech-owl and Kestrel Box

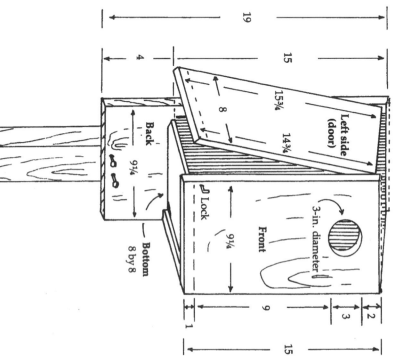

Instructions

A. 1. Lay out, mark, and saw out all the parts.

2. On the back panel, drill a ½-in. hole, centered 2 in. down from the top.

3. On the front panel, cut out the 3-in. entrance, centered 2 in. down from the top, as shown.

4. Bevel ⅛ in. off the back and front pieces to fit the roof slant.

5. Across the interior surface of the back, 4 in. up from the bottom, draw a line, extending it across the edges and the weather surface. Draw another line across the interior surface of the right side panel, 1 in. up from the bottom, and extend it across the edges. Do the same with the front panel.

6. If the wood is smooth, roughen the interior surfaces of the front and side panels with the corner of the rasp, scratching hard across the grain.

7. Put 2 nails into the right side, to come out ¼ in. below the line on the interior surface. Set the bottom on edge. Match the line on the right side panel with the interior surface of the bottom panel. Push both pieces flush against a wall, and drive the nails part way in.

8. Turn the unit on its side edge. Put 2 nails into the back to connect with the edge of the right side panel. Match the marks as you fit the 2 pieces together. Drive the nails part way in. Check to see if the back extends ¼ in. above the side panel. Line up the bottom, hold, and drive 2 nails part way in. If everything fits, drive in all the nails.

9. Place the front in position, matching the marks. See if it extends ¼ in. above the right side panel. Put 2 nails into the side and 2 into the bottom. Check the alignment, then drive them all in.

10. Slip the other side in place to check for fit. Draw a horizontal line, 1 in. from the top, across the weather surface. Put 1 nail through the front panel and 1 nail through the back panel, at either end of the line. Drill a hole near the bottom for the nail—a 1½-in. galvanized nail or right-angle screw hook.

11. Run a strip of caulking compound along the beveled edge of the back panel. Position the roof so it is flush with the back and has an equal overhang on each side. Put 2 nails in back and 2 in front.

B. 1. To mount this box, drive a sixteen-penny galvanized nail into the place you have chosen for the box, being sure that it hangs 10 to 30 ft. above the ground. Hook the house on this nail, through the ½-in. hole in back, then drive 2 galvanized siding nails part way through the back, where it extends beneath the bottom. Leave the nails sticking out enough that you can pull them out easily when changing locations.

B.

Hole ½-in. diameter

Sixteen-penny nail

Post or snag mount

Barn owl Box

Compared with a wren house, a barn owl box is huge—rather like a civic auditorium. However, it's easy to build. Just be sure you have plenty of material. And be fairly certain that there is a barn owl or two in your neighborhood. Otherwise, the box may wind up as cozy quarters for starlings.

Materials

Cedar or exterior plywood, ⅝ in., 50½ by 34½ in.; or T 1-11 siding scraps:

    Bottom—18 by 15 in.
    Sides (2)—each 18 by 15 in.
    Back—16¼ by 16 in.
    Front—16¼ by 16 in.
Roof—plywood door skin or masonite, ⅛ in., 21¼ by 18¼ in.
Fourpenny galvanized box nails
Right-angle screw hooks (3), 1½ in. long
Bracket—exterior plywood, ⅝ in., 32¼ by 16½ in.; or T 1-11 siding

Braces (2)—wood, 1 by 4 by 16¼ in.
Flathead screws (2), 1 in. long, ³⁄₁₆ in. in diameter
Wood (optional), 10 by 18 by ¾ in.
Screws (optional, 4), 1⅛ in. long
Wood (optional), 2 by 4 in., 2 or 3 ft. long
Sixteen-penny galvanized framing nail (optional)

Tools

Square	Pencil
Ruler	Saw
Thin wire or cord, 36 in. long	Compass, or 6-in. saucer
Keyhole saw	Plane
Brace, with ⅝- and 1-in. bits	Hammer
Screwdriver	Rasp
Countersink	

Instructions

A. 1. Cut the bottom, 15 by 18 in., and saw off the corners ¾ in. back. Cut the sides to the same dimensions as the bottom, and cut the roof (made out of ⅛-in. plywood or masonite) to 18¼ by 21¼ in.

2. Near the top edge of the wood you are using for the front panel, draw a line 16¼ in. across. Bring one 16-in. line down at 90 degrees from each end of this line. Connect the bottom ends of these 2 lines with a horizontal line.

3. Next, draw a line, parallel to and centered between the first 2 vertical lines, 16 in. upward from the horizontal line. Make a mark at the top of this line. Extend this same vertical line 18 in. below and at right angles to the horizontal line. Now, make a mark 15 in. up each of the vertical side lines.

4. With a pencil tied to a thin wire or cord that does not stretch, you can swing an arc across the center top mark, intersecting those on each side. At the bottom end of the 18-in. vertical line, place your thumbnail on the wire, 33 in. down from the pencil. Try a few swings, with the pencil held vertically so you can check its passage over the 3 marks. Make small adjustments and draw a curved line intersecting all 3 marks. This forms the shape of the roof.

A. Barn owl Box

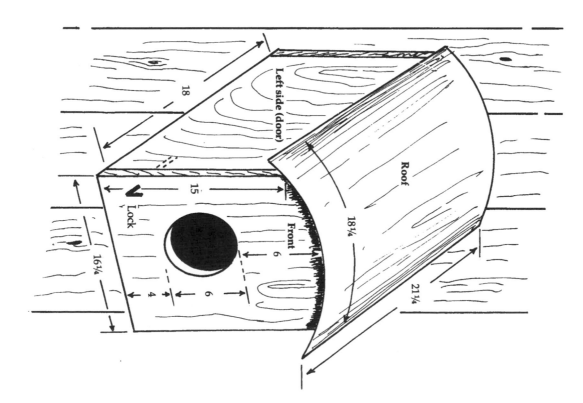

Note: Dimensions are in inches

5. The bottom edge of the entrance is 4 in. up. Use a compass or a 6-in. saucer to inscribe the circle.

6. Cut out the front panel, using a keyhole saw for the 6-in. entrance. Round off the edges with a rasp. Use this panel as a pattern for cutting out the back, omitting the entrance hole, of course.

7. Bevel the top of the sides ⅛ in. Drill 3 holes, ⅝ in. in diameter, just beneath the bevel and evenly spaced on both sides. These are vent holes.

8. Put 2 nails in the bottom edge of the right side panel. Set the bottom panel on edge. Push both pieces flush against the wall, making the side panel flush with the bottom. Drive in the nails.

9. Turn the unit on its side edge. Put 2 nails in the back to connect with the edge of the right side panel. Align the back with the side, then drive in the nails.

10. Place 2 nails in the right side of the front panel and 2 nails in the bottom edge. Place the panel in position and drive in the nails.

11. Check the fit of the left side. Then draw a horizontal line, 1 in. from the top, across the weather surface. Put a 1½-in. right-angle screw hook through the front and back panels where the line intersects them. Drill a small hole through the bottom of the front piece, and insert a 1½-in. right-angle screw hook, which will serve as the lock nail. (Although you will probably make infrequent inspections, you should always make provisions for opening a bird box.)

12. The roof has such a shallow curve, you should have no problem putting it together. Place it with equal overhang, front and back, and with 1 in. extending over the right side to which you are going to nail. Drive 2 nails part way into the right side. (If you are using ⅛-in. plywood door skin, be sure the outside grain runs parallel to the length of the box. It bends more easily that way.) Start 2 nails on the left side, into the front and back pieces, not the movable side panel. Check the alignment and drive the nails in. Place a few more nails where necessary.

13. It's difficult to tell if barn owls prefer raw wood or painted surfaces. Whether or not you paint the outside or stain it to blend with the surroundings is entirely up to you. But be sure to allow several days for the fumes to wear off if you don't leave it as raw wood.

B. 1. Some people prefer to build a bracket or shelf to which they can fasten their barn owl box. It is fairly simple to build. First, measure out a rectangle 14 by 16 in. and cut it on the diagonal, corner to corner. These are the sides.

2. Cut out the top piece. Cut the 1 by 4 into 2 pieces 16¾ in. long. Stand one piece on edge and nail on the top, flush with the back.

3. Nail on the sides flush with the top and its back edge.

4. Nail in the bottom brace about 1 in. from the bottom corners of the sides. Now you can nail the bracket high on the barn wall through the braces.

C. 1. With the box tight against the wall and on the bracket, drill and countersink two holes for the flathead screws underneath to hold it.

Bracket

B.

Top brace

Right side

Top   18

16¾

Bottom brace

Left side

16

14

16¾

4

1

Note: Dimensions are in inches

2. A more convenient method is the one used with the Wood Duck Box. First, place a 10 by 18 by ¾-in. board against the box, tucking the board underneath the roof overhang so that the board extends about 3 in. below the bottom. Countersink the holes and use 4 screws to fasten the board to the back. Through the board and the box, center and drill a 1-in. hole, 2 in. down from the top.

3. On the place you have selected for the box, nail two 2 by 4-in. blocks of wood, each 12 in. long, so they are horizontal, 16 in. apart, and parallel. Near the top edge of the upper block, center and drive in a sixteen-penny nail, angled slightly downward, until about 2 in. of it sticks out. Now hook the box in place. Drive 2 nails into the lower block through the board that extends beneath the bottom panel. Leave these nails sticking out slightly so you can easily relocate the box if needed.

Suggestions

Enticing owls and kestrels to use nest boxes first requires that your place be near suitable habitat for each species. Here are some other pointers that may prove helpful.

c.

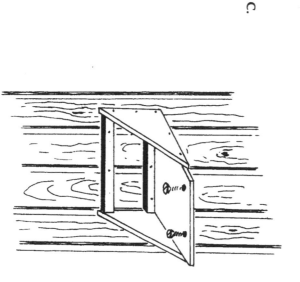

1. For owls, sprinkle two inches of wood chips in the bottom of the box. These birds are accustomed to natural nest cavities with debris in the bottom. Neither the screech-owl nor the barn owl is a highly sophisticated nest builder. In fact, the barn owl builds a miserable nest—a few wood chips against which it leans the eggs. Nevertheless, wood chips will enhance the box's acceptability (as it does for wood ducks)—owls recognize posh nesting quarters.

2. Remember that fur pellets on the ground indicate a favorite roosting place up above for an owl. If it is a tree that is free of limbs, nine to 12 feet up, try it for a screech-owl nest box location. Sometimes a screech-owl will nest in a box under the eaves of an outbuilding. Pellets should tell you where.

3. Barn owls prefer lofts in large buildings or old silos. Again, watch for disgorged pellets on the ground as an indication of favored spots.

4. It doesn't hurt to put up several boxes in likely locations to give the birds a choice.

5. With kestrels, first watch them to determine their favorite perches. Then mount your boxes in the open, on posts, 10 to 12 feet above the ground. Use a post- or pole-mounted baffle to prevent predators from getting to the nest box.

6. Until you are sure the kestrel accommodation is being used, place the post or pole it is mounted on in a hole, staked and nailed to angle braces to hold it steady. Once you decide to set the post permanently in cement, make sure you do not mount it too high for regular nest checks. Some landlords prefer to use a 14-foot stepladder for this chore. Others prefer to buy or build a pulley system for raising and lowering the box during nest monitoring visits. Pulleys allow the box to be lowered safely without tipping it over and possibly disturbing the box's precious contents.

Shelf Nest Specialists

Nesting Shelves for Robins, Phoebes, Barn Swallows, and Song Sparrows

Not all birds are hole nesters that will live in birdhouses. Some birds nest on tree limbs, in shrubs, or on beams. Those that nest on beams are more easily attracted to shelves, although proper design, location, and luck may allow success with some of the others. Shelf nests are often a big hit with birdhouse builders—and former bird-house builders. Half a dozen shelves often can be knocked together in the time it takes to build one of the complicated birdhouses. And the birds the shelves attract are as fascinating as those that choose houses.

Barn swallows are perhaps the shelf nest specialists you can most easily attract if you live near water, such as a pond or lake.

The barn swallow is the only swallow that has a deeply forked tail. Its underparts are salmon colored and its back is a dark, pur-plish shade. A kind of gurgling burble is its distinctive call, often ending in a series of clicks. Tiny flying insects, such as midges and flies, satisfy its enormous appetite.

Ranging throughout most of the United States and wintering from South America to Mexico, these six-inch birds arrive in their nesting areas around mid-April, depending on the latitude. Their nest construction is an engineering triumph. Beginning with a tiny splotch of mud stuck to the wall, the nest seems to grow in a series of expanding, concentric semicircles, of mud mixed with straw until a cupped nest is formed. The parents then line it with feathers. The four to five eggs the female lays are white with reddish or brown spots. Usually, two broods are raised per nesting season. The fledgling barn swallows' introduction to flight training occurs when they are teased into tumbling from the nest. During the first several evenings, the parents coax them back into the nest for safe keeping.

Another shelf nester you may attract is the **eastern phoebe,** which migrates to its nesting area early in the year and stays late. Occasionally, some will remain all winter. Generally gray in color, without the eye ring or distinct wing bars that distinguish other flycatchers, the eastern phoebe ranges generally east of the Rockies from southern Canada, throughout the eastern part of the United States.

Often found near running water, this seven-inch flycatcher has responded favorably to civilization wherever buildings, especially in the country, afford a flat surface for nesting. Like the barn swallow, the eastern phoebe makes a nest of mud in which it lays five pure white eggs. Normally, two broods are raised.

The **American robin** is found throughout the United States and Canada, as far north as there are trees. Some robins stay throughout the winter, even in northern parts of the continent. Its population numbers have increased near agricultural areas and in cities where broad lawns afford excellent opportunities for searching out worms and grubs. This hardy bird is nearly 10 inches long and displays an orange breast. The female is somewhat grayer than the black-backed male.

Robins make nests by plastering twigs and stems together with mud. For a nesting site, they favor an evergreen or a support beam that shelters the nest from rain. Their three to five eggs are blue green, and they raise two broods. The parents defend their territories with considerable vigor, sometimes fighting their own reflections in a window. Gauze or plastic, dropped over the window to cut the reflection, should stop the altercations.

An eastern phoebe.

One of the most delightful of the shelf nesters is the **song sparrow**. When you first hear its melodious song, you will find it hard to believe that it is coming from this six-inch chap—reddish brown on the back with dark, vertical stripes underneath. In fact, if you had never heard the song, you might just think of the song sparrow as "that little brown bird in the backyard."

Found from southern Alaska and Canada, south throughout most of the United States, this bird spends the winter from southern Canada, south through Florida and the Gulf Coast. It favors brushy zones, usually near water, delivering its song from the topmost branch of a thicket or brush pile.

An early nester, the song sparrow raises two broods—the first, hidden near a thicket in matted grass of the previous year; the second, higher up as the summer foliage becomes dense. Usually the parents build the second nest only four feet off the ground. They lay four greenish white eggs that are blotched with brown.

Shelf for Barn Swallows, Phoebes, and Robins

This first shelf is easy to construct and will be used by barn swallows. Phoebes or robins may be attracted if you add two inches to the dimensions of each piece. Since it is so easy to build, you will not mind making two or three. Then you can put shelves up in different locations, increasing your chances of having nesting families.

Materials

Cedar boards or exterior plywood, $5/8$ in., $25\frac{3}{4}$ by $8\frac{1}{4}$ in.; or T 1-11 siding scraps:

Bottom—6 by 6 in.
Sides (2)—each $6\frac{5}{8}$ by 6 in.
Back—6 by 8 in.
Fourpenny galvanized box nails
Tenpenny galvanized box nails (3)

Tools

Square
Pencil
Ruler
Saw and Keyhole saw
Plane
Brace, with $\frac{1}{2}$-in. bit
Hammer

Instructions

A. 1. With a square and pencil, lay out and mark the parts according to the dimensions shown in the drawing, then saw out all the pieces. If you do not have a sharp keyhole saw to cut the curve in the end pieces, then make the alternate side pieces, cutting off the corners 2 in. out from the top and 2 in. up from the bottom, as shown. Plane off any splinters.

2. Mark a horizontal line along the face of the back panel, 2 in. up from the bottom. Drill a $\frac{1}{2}$-in. hole, centered in the back and 1 in. down from the top.

3. On the back side (the side that will go against the wall) of the back panel, start 2 nails so they will come out $\frac{1}{4}$ in. above the line on the other side. Then nail the bottom to the back so that the edges are flush and the underside of the bottom rests on the line drawn on the back piece.

A.

Alternate shape for side pieces

Note: Dimensions are in inches

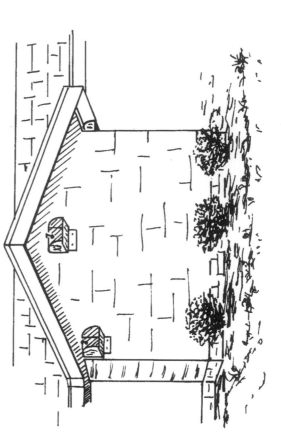

C.

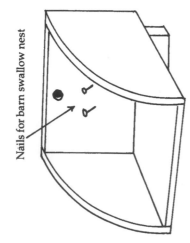

Nails for barn swallow nest

B.

4. Start 2 nails in the right side to connect with the edge of the bottom piece. Start another nail in the side panel, 1½ in. from the top, to connect with the back panel. Align the side piece with the bottom and back panels, being sure the edges are flush. Now drive in all the nails. Repeat with the left side panel.

B. 1. One observer has noticed that barn swallows often anchor their nests to nails on the side of a beam. If you want to test this idea, then put 2 nails into the back panel, about 2 in. apart and 2 in. up from the bottom. Leave 1¾ in. of the nails sticking out.

C. 1. This shelf nest should be tacked high under the eaves—8 to 12 ft. for swallows, 6 to 15 ft. for phoebes. Drive a tenpenny box nail into the desired location, leaving ¾ in. of the nail protruding. Hook the shelf onto the nail, through the ½-in. hole in the back of the shelf. Where the back extends below the bottom, drive 2 more siding nails into the back, leaving enough of the nails sticking out so you can pull them easily if you want to try new locations.

Song Sparrow Shelf Nest

The song sparrow insists on having a shelf that is open on four sides. Perhaps this is due to its strong sense of territory—it constantly keeps a lookout for trespassers. Or perhaps it is because of its need to watch for danger. Like many thicket dwellers, this bird depends on secrecy of the nest location for protecting itself and its young against predators.

Materials

Cedar boards, or exterior plywood, ⅝ in., 17¼ by 16¾ in.; or T 1-11 siding scraps

Bottom—6 by 6 in.

Sides (2)—each 7¼ by 1½ in.

Back—6 by 6 in.

Front—6 by 6 in.

Roof, left side—9 by 5¾ in.

Roof, right side—9 by 5⅝ in.

Fourpenny galvanized box nails

Wood, 2 by 2 by 4 in.

Caulking compound

Wire (optional)

Post (optional), 2 in. by 4 in. by 5 ft. or galvanized 1½-in. pipe 10- ft. length

Tools

Square

Pencil

Ruler

Compass or small jar lid

Keyhole saw

Saw

Plane

Hammer

Instructions

A. 1. Lay out and mark all the parts. Use a compass or a lid from a small jar to outline the arch. Be sure when you cut out the arches with a keyhole saw that the posts are left 1½ in. wide.

2. Saw out all the parts. Cut off the corners of the bottom panel back ¼ in. Plane off the splinters.

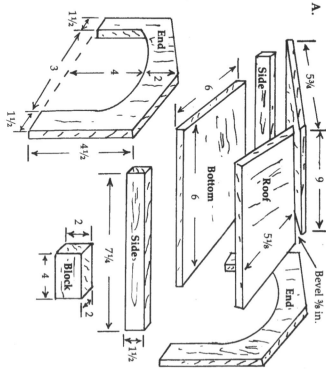

A.

Note: Dimensions are in inches

B.

C.

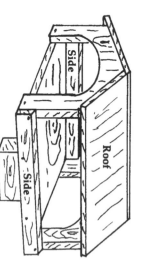

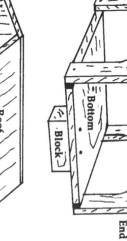

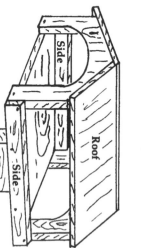

B. 1. On an end panel, start one nail about ¼ in. from the bottom of each post. Align the end piece so it is flush with the bottom, then drive in the nails. Repeat with the other end panel.

2. Next, nail the wooden block to the bottom panel, flush with one edge, as shown. This will give you the option of nailing the shelf to a post.

C. 1. On 1 side piece, start 2 nails, about ¼ in. up from the bottom edge and 2 in. in from each end. Align the side with the bottom and end pieces so the edges are flush. Drive in the nails. Place 1 nail through the top of the side into each end post. Be careful not to break the arched end piece. Hang it over the edge of the workbench for support as you nail. Repeat with the other side piece.

2. Bevel ⅜ in. off the top edge of the smaller half of the roof and set it in place with equal overhang front and back. Start 2 nails 1½ in. down from the peak to connect with the ends. Tack the nails to hold.

3. Put the other roof section in place to check the tightness of the fit. You may need to make adjustments. Then bevel ⅜ in. off the top edge. Start 2 nails, 1½ in. down from the top, to connect with the end panels.

4. Run a strip of caulking compound along the top edge of the first roof section beveled. Lay on the second half and tack it to hold. Check the fit and alignment, then drive in all the nails. Drive one more nail into the caulked edge near the center.

5. You can wire this shelf inside a thicket or mount it on a low post, well hidden by heavy cover.

Suggestions

Shelf nesters are specialists, often displaying a preference for locations that we consider to be outlandish. But nesting is their business, so try to observe their preferences. You will have to experiment in order to be successful. Meanwhile here are a few suggestions, first about barn swallows, then robins, phoebes, and song sparrows.

1. Barn swallows normally prefer something tucked high under the eaves, near the peak of a roof and against a wall. They even will nest in similar places inside an open building. Provide a number of shelf nests in suitable locations so the swallows can make a choice. Lure them away from areas you don't want soiled—they do leave droppings—or try for locations over the planter strip where droppings might do some good. If there is a sidewalk directly beneath, place the shelves at the outer edge of the overhang, tucked just inside the trim board, or install "splash boards" beneath, to protect unsuspecting guests.

2. Do not overlook the garage as a possibility for barn swallow shelf locations, or a breezeway if there is a planter strip beneath. But don't get the idea that you will dictate all nesting sites. For example, one pair insisted on a nest inside a garage. Daily, the owner was summoned to open the garage door slightly, so they could feed their young. And keep in mind that if your lakeshore home is surrounded by trees, the barn swallows are not likely to penetrate at all. They prefer open areas around buildings.

3. Barn swallows will nest in colonies, but not at first, so keep the shelves spaced apart—every six feet or so. During the years that follow, you can try them closer together.

4. It does not hurt to have a good source of mud handy. This helps to speed up nest construction. Spade up about a three-by five-foot section of dirt and keep it thoroughly watered. Stick a few white feathers around to help the birds discover the mud. You also will need to supply additional white feathers, because they are the favorite lining for barn, tree, and violet-green swallow nests.

5. Unhook the shelf nests in the fall after the last brood is gone. Scrub the shelves with a mild bleach-water solution, hose them off, and store them for the next season.

6. Robins often nested on support beams of porches found on older homes in the 1920s. Try putting shelf nests at the corners of your house—under the eaves and near the downspouts. The transverse arm of a downspout is often a perching place for the

neighborhood robins—they are less likely to overlook your shelf if it's there.

7. As with barn swallows, it's a good idea to put up several shelves for robins. It gives them a choice and enhances the chances of a shelf being discovered.

8. If a robin nests on a shelf, clean the nest off at the end of the season, take the shelf down, clean it, and store it until the next nesting season.

9. Since phoebes often nest on bridge beams or farm outbuildings that have similar structures, you might try nailing a single, long board six inches wide under the eaves. In some cases, phoebes have been reported nesting year after year on the same shelf, building a new nest alongside the old one each season.

10. Watching the area around your bird feeder during the winter will tell you if it is even worth trying to attract song sparrows to one of your shelves.

11. If you do decide to put up song sparrow shelf nests, place two or three of them in thickets around your backyard. One may prove suitable to a song sparrow pair. With their strong territorial sense, it is unlikely that you will find more than one pair in close proximity. Since song sparrows insist on nesting close to the ground, you need to choose a thicket where the shelf will be well hidden. Wire it in place, one to three feet off the ground. If the shelf is accepted, then you will probably get a second brood.

Predators & Competitors

Some of your most frustrating moments as a landlord for birds will be caused by predators and competitors. These persistent pests can drive away your most prized guests or kill those that stay. The devices described in this chapter should help you solve many of the problems. But others will arise, calling you—as always—to exercise your ingenuity in providing homes and food for your birds.

By far, your most vexing problems with birdhouses will occur because of **house sparrows** or **starlings**, depending on the entrance size of your birdhouses. house sparrows seem almost vindictive—if not that, at least thorough. When occupying a swallow house, for example, they will peck holes in the eggs, throw out the material, and even kill young swallows that are ready to fly. Starlings damage eggs or build nests on top of the eggs. You need to discourage or remove these two pests in the early season in order to improve your chances of nesting success.

The sparrow traps described in this chapter are designed for quick-release swallow houses such as the one described in this book. Both traps are removable so that the birdhouse can be used by nesting swallows once you have taken care of the intruders. Although these traps will not work for a bottom entry house, they can be adapted to fit almost any with a side entrance. A word of caution though: Do not set a sparrow trap unless you can check it hourly. Never leave it set during your absence.

Starlings, too, can be trapped in birdhouses with holes large enough to admit them (two inches in diameter and more), but in some areas they are so numerous that you may find yourself overwhelmed. Other methods to discourage them, such as shiny interiors, are mentioned in the chapter about purple martins. So, we'll talk about sparrow-trapping with the idea that some of these methods may be adapted in a few cases to starling problems.

Although you might be tempted to take drastic action with every house sparrow you catch, there is a harmless way to keep each one from becoming a problem again, especially if you do not wish to take on the role of sparrow or starling exterminator. First, place a captured bird in a fine-mesh bag.

Take your captive at least 12 miles out in the country, far from your nest boxes. If you are curious about the bird's ability to refind your nestboxes, you might dab a bright spot of latex paint on its tail. If it returns, which is unlikely, you'll know that the next trip must be many more miles—after a few rounds of this, if you have a very determined house sparrow, the role of exterminator may not seem so unthinkable.

Male house sparrows are the nest-site competitors. Removing a male is always best. Discouraged, the female will drift elsewhere. But if you trap the female, the male sparrow will simply find another and put her to work. Then you'll be in for it again!

Two other ways of handling the house sparrow and starling problem are still in the experimental stage, but are looking promising. Apparently these birds do not like bright interiors. Birdhouses fashioned out of plastic bottles and milk jugs do not appeal to them, but many desirable species find them quite suitable.

House sparrows can outcompete other cavity nesters.

Predator Guards

When you put houses or feeders on tree trunks or posts, remember to install predator guards. Otherwise, your efforts may be wasted. Mounted directly beneath and surrounding the post or tree, three basic kinds are effective. One is a metal cone flared about 10–16 inches in diameter. The second is a metal sleeve about four feet long. Both types surround the post or tree and prevent climbing predators such as cats, raccoons, and opossums from reaching the nest.

The very best predator baffle is the pole-mounted stovepipe baffle described in this chapter. Properly placed it is too slick for climbing snakes and wobbles too much for mammal predators to get a foothold for climbing.

If you mount houses and other conveniences away from trees, buildings, and other possible crossover accesses for predators, predator guards mounted below will give enough protection. However, in a small yard or other area where this is impossible, you could install a cone-shaped guard eighteen inches above as well as below. Some people do this to keep squirrels from getting at bird feeders and nest boxes.

Baffle walls are another method of protecting birds from predators. Forming an L-shaped passage, they help prevent hawks and owls from reaching the nest area with their talons, especially when a porch block (such as the one in purple martin houses) enables these predators to perch at the birdhouse entrance. Swallows do not mind zigzagging to reach the nest. Neither do martins.

Baffle blocks offer protection in a similar way. Adding extra thickness to the entrance wall, they make it difficult for the predator to reach far enough inside to devour any egg or young bird. Although the baffle wall in the drawings was designed for the martin houses described in this book, the principle can be adapted to almost any birdhouse with enough wall space at the entrance, provided it does not crowd the nest area.

Drop–Board Sparrow Trap

This trap can be used to capture house sparrows alive in any of the nest boxes we've described using the 1½-inch entrance.

Materials

Trigger—wire coat hanger
Support block—siding, ⅝ by 2 by 1 in
Fourpenny box nails

Eye screws (2)
Drop board—wood, 1 by 8 by 2½ in.
Roundhead screw, 1 in. long
Exterior latex paint, white
Rubber sponge, 1 by 3 by 5 in.

Tools

Pliers, 2 pairs	Ruler
Square	Pencil
Hammer	Triangle
Drill, with assorted small bits	Screwdriver
Saw	Paintbrush

Instructions

A. 1. First, let's make the trigger. (This is a little tricky—read steps 1 through 4 before you start shaping the trigger.) Use pliers to straighten the coat hanger wire. Hold the wire horizontal and parallel to your body. Starting with the right-hand end of the wire, bend ¼ in. of it out and away from you, forming a tight U shape. Make a 90-degree bend ¼ in. from the closed end of the

Drop Board Sparrow Trap

A.

Wire trigger

B.

Chickadee escape · Back · Support block ⅝ by 2 by 1 · Swing · Drop board · 8 · 2½

5. Slip the vertical arm of the trigger under the eye screws. Hold it with a keeper nail—a fourpenny box nail—tacked at a slight slant and centered on the side of the eye screw openings. If the slant is too much, you may have to bend the nail upward to clear the end of the drop board. Tack this nail deep enough to hold but shallow enough to be removed with pliers and reset when needed.

6. In the 8 by 2½-in. drop board, drill a hole, centered vertically and ½ in. from one end. Slip in a screw that is 1 in. long and slightly smaller than the hole.

7. Make a mark 4 in. down from the top edge of the house and 2⅞ in. from the left edge. Put the screw through the hole in the drop board and align the screw with the mark. Now test the drop board position by holding the screw as you let the board

U so it ends up being faced away from you. After ½ in. from this last bend, make another 90-degree turn out and away from you.

2. After another ½ in., make a 90-degree bend so the unbent end of the wire faces downward. After about 3 in., bend the wire at a 90-degree angle so the unbent end of the wire faces right. After ½ in., bend the unbent portion of the wire another 90 degrees away from you.

3. After 4 in., bend the wire back toward you, making a U shape about 1 in. wide between the parallel sides. Make the right side of the U shape about 3 in. long. Then bend the wire back away from you in a similar U. Snip off about 2 in. from the last bend.

4. Take your finished wire creation and sight down the vertical arm. Make sure the 90-degree angles at the top and bottom of the arm line up. You may have to twist the top one a little to come beneath the drop board when the trigger is locked in place.

B. 1 Now take the support block and start 2 nails ½ in. from each end of it. Place the support block on the interior surface of the floor of the house, against the front wall under the entrance hole, 1¼ in. from the interior surface of the right side. Drive the nails all the way in. Clinch them if they protrude on the front.

2. Using the triangle, on the interior surface of the swallow house's entrance panel, make pencil marks to use as guides for placing the trigger. Draw the first line so it is parallel to the floor, extending from the left just under the entrance. Mark the second line parallel to the first, 2½ in. down from the top, extending from the left so that it goes above the entrance.

3. Next, run a vertical line ⅜ in. from the left edge of the entrance. Extend it to intersect both parallel lines.

4. Open two eye screws and set them into the wood on the vertical line, ⅛ in. inside the points where the parallel lines intersect the vertical line. Turn the screws until the opened sections face right, toward the entrance. Twist them in deep enough to hold, with just enough space for the coat hanger wire to slip easily underneath.

swing in an arc across the entrance hole. The board should clear the trigger hardware by ⅛ in. when the wire loops are swung outward.

8. When you have found the proper arc, set the screw part way in and test the trigger. The wire should barely come underneath the end of the board in order to hold it up. Make tiny adjustments by bending the trigger wire. The board should drop with the slightest possible outward swing of the loops. Adjust the keeper nail so that the trigger swings freely.

9. On the drop board, saw a narrow, V-shaped notch up from the bottom to the hole for the screw. Set the screw permanency, but not so it is too tight. The drop board must swing up and down easily and must be easily removed from the screw when you want to move it.

10. Paint the end of the drop board white. This way you can tell at a glance whether or not the trap has been sprung.

11. It is best if you build a trigger mechanism for each box and keep the drop board inside when you do not need it for trapping. Lay it flat, held by a sponge, doubled and shoved beneath the serpentined loops. The birds can use it for nesting. If sparrows evict the swallows, clean out the nest material, set the drop board, trap the sparrows, and again make the box available to the swallows.

Drop-Door Sparrow Trap

If your birdhouse has little side-wall space but enough over the entrance, you can install a drop-door sparrow trap. The principle for bending the trigger wire is similar to that described in the instructions for the drop-board sparrow trap. However, the sliding door is made of masonite.

Once installed, the drop-door may be difficult to take out if you want to use the box for a birdhouse as well. This can be overcome by drilling a small hole and inserting a short screw through the wall and the door in the open position. The trigger mechanism can be immobilized by wedging a sponge between the serpentined loops and the floor.

The dimensions fit the quick-release swallow box described earlier, but can be altered to fit birdhouses with larger entrances if wall space above is sufficient to accommodate the door. Once it is adjusted, this device is faster than the drop-board, and it can be set by tipping the birdhouse upside down to get the door positioned. Then, by slowly rotating the birdhouse upright, the trigger will fall, ready, into place.

Materials

Door stop—wood, ⅜ by 1½ by 19 in.
Wire nails (10), #18, ¾ in. long
Door—masonite, ¼ in., 1¾ by 2 in.
Small eye screws (2)
Wire coat hanger
Exterior latex paint, white

Tools

Triangle	Pencil
Ruler	Saw
Plane	Sandpaper
Hammer	Pliers, 2 pairs
Paintbrush	

Instructions

1. Using the triangle and pencil, mark two vertical lines inside, ¼ in. from the entrance edges on each side, from top to bottom.

2. Lay the triangle flat against the inside and draw a line crossing the others at a right angle, touching the bottom edge of the entrance.

3. With the saw, rip the length of the door stop, 1 in. wide. Cut off two lengths, 4¼ in. Plane the sawed edges lightly and lay aside.

4. Cut two more lengths, 3¼ in. Plane and set aside.

5. Cut a length, 4 in, and plane.

6. On the lines you drew, begin to frame around the entrance, first the 4-in. piece across the bottom, using the 3¾-in. nails; then nail the 3¼-inches up the sides. Be careful that these remain exactly parallel.

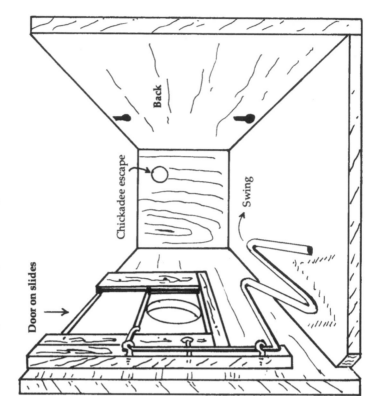

Drop Board Sparrow Trap

7. From masonite, cut out the door—2 in. wide, 1¾ in. long. Sand down the edges and check for fit. There should be about ½₂ in. clearance on each side.

8. Place the birdhouse upright to see if the door drops without sticking. If it sticks, sand the edges of the door again.

9. To form a slot for the door, nail the 4¼-in. cleats over the 3¼-in. members, but let them overhang ¼ in. toward ¼ toward the center. Try the door again to see if it drops smoothly.

10. Now for the trigger. Using the triangle against the bottom, draw a vertical line up the right-hand cleat, ⅜ in. from the edge nearest the door.

11. Place the door in the slot, its bottom edge even with the upper edge of the entrance, and mark across the vertical line. Make another cross mark 2¼ in. below.

12. Start a nail at these points. Open the eye screws enough to admit the coat hanger wire, and twist them into place, the opened sides toward the entrance.

13. Hold the coat hanger wire vertically in front of you with a pair of pliers. Using the other pliers, grasp the wire 2 in. down from the top and bend it toward you, a sharp 90 degrees. Grasp the wire again, ½ in. nearer, and start a bend to the right in a gentle C shape about 1 in. wide.

14. Measure down 2⅜ in. from the first bend you made at the top. Holding the wire as before, but at that point, use both pliers to bend it toward you from below at a sharp 90 degrees, keeping the direction in line with the first bend at the top and parallel to it.

15. One-half inch toward you, bend the wire to the right, 90 degrees, horizontally. Grasp the wire 4 in. out from that point and bend it back toward you, bringing it around into a U-shaped loop to the left about 1 in. wide. At 3 in., make another U-shaped loop to the right, creating a series of parallel loops 1 to 1½ in. wide toward you horizontally. Snip off the wire 2 in. from the last bend.

16. Slip the vertical shaft under the eye screw openings. The serpentined loops at the bottom should hang about 1½ in.. above the floor and swing freely after the eye screws are pinched shut.

17. Adjust the C-shaped curve at the top. You may have to snip off some. It should barely come beneath the drop door when the trigger is set, and it should release the door on the slightest outward swing of the loops. Test it. Twist the vertical shaft until things line up properly.

Stovepipe Predator Baffle

Many backyard bird landlords have successfully protected their housing from predators using the pole-mounted stovepipe baffle shown at right. The galvanized metal stovepipe is slick and therefore hard to climb for snakes and raccoons. The way it is mounted at the top only allows the bottom of the stovepipe to swing freely back and forth when a predator tries to gain purchase. Hardware cloth inside the baffle prevents access to the box up the pole. Greasing the pole and baffle can make this set up even more effective.

Materials

Galvanized pipe ¾-in. inside diameter
Strapping brackets
Weatherproof screws (to mount box to pole)
Hardware cloth (½-in. mesh)
Machine screws with nuts
Hanger iron (in two 7-in. strips)
Galvanized stovepipe (24-in. x 7-in.).

Tools

Tinsnips
Screwdriver

Instructions

1. With tinsnips, cut the hardware cloth into a circle 8 inches in diameter. Place it over the stovepipe, bending the edges down so that it will fit snugly into the pipe, about an inch down from the top (A). Close any gaps between hardware cloth and stovepipe, otherwise snakes may squeeze through.

2. Next, use tinsnips to cut three tabs (B) in the top of the stovepipe. Bend these over the hardware cloth. Cut a small hole in the middle of the cloth to allow the assembly to slip over the box mounting pipe.

3. Bolt the two strips of hanger iron (C) securely on either side of the mounting pipe, and bend them to support the hardware cloth. Duct tape wrapped around the pole helps hold the hanger iron in place. Slip the assembled baffle over the hanger iron bracket, just below the nest box. It should wobble a little, which further discourages climbing predators.

JULIE ZICKEFOOSE

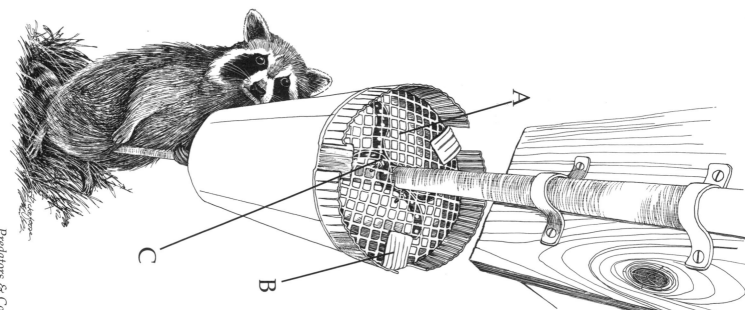

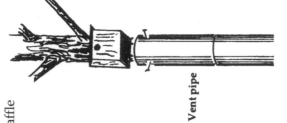

A.

Vent pipe

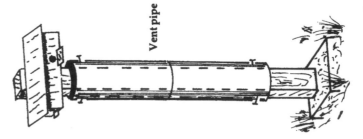

B.

Vent pipe

Sleeve–Type Predator Baffle

The easiest of the predator baffles to install is the sleeve type, which uses two sections of aluminum or galvanized stove or vent pipe. This material comes in opened sections and can be interlocked around a tree or post as long as the metal sections are large enough for flexing.

Materials
Aluminum or galvanized vent pipe, 2 lengths, each 24 in. long
Tenpenny galvanized box nails (4)

Tools
Hammer

Instructions
A. 1. Pop the two lengths of vent pipe together around the tree you have selected for your birdhouse. Tack four nails along the overlap as shown. Leave enough sticking out to make adjustments as the tree grows and to allow air circulation around the trunk.

2. If the tree is too large, you can buy lightweight, galvanized sheet metal (tin) in rolls 24 in. wide. Measure the circumference of the tree, allowing 2 or 3 extra inches for a loose fit. Be sure to get enough for 2 sections.

3. Measure out the circumference and cut the sheet metal into two equal "wrap-around" lengths.

4. Place the lower length 23 in. below the birdhouse with about a 1-in. overlap. Along this seam, place one nail 2 in. down from the top, one in the center, and one about 2 in. from the bottom.

5. Now wrap the upper section, tucked under the birdhouse with a 1-in. overlap vertically along the trunk, and overlapping the bottom section about 1 in. Tack 3 nails along the seam as you did with the bottom. Jiggle or pry the circumference so that the metal will stand away from the trunk to allow air circulation.

B. 1. If you will be mounting your birdhouse on a post, assemble the sleeves first. Then slip them over the post and tack them in place before mounting the birdhouse.

A.

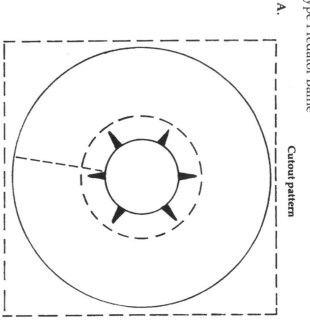

Cutout pattern

B.

Metal Cone

Metal Cone

Cone-Type Predator Baffle

With plenty of yard space this cone-shaped predator guard is another type that can be used effectively to protect young birds in the nest. One may also be installed above the birdhouse on trees too near buildings or other structures that might allow the predator to cross over and gain access to the nest.

Materials

Sheet of galvanized metal, 24 by 24 in.
Fourpenny galvanized box nails
Small panhead, sheet metal screws (4)

Tools

Pencil
String, 13 in. long
Pliers
Hammer
Drill, with metal-cutting bits

Ruler
Tin snips
C clamp
Screwdriver

Baffle Walls for Trio-Unit Martin House

Although rare, there may be an occasion when a hawk or owl reaches through a nestbox entrance to devour the young. The nine-inch depth of the trio-unit martin house provides a little protection. But if problems occur, these baffle walls will help to cut losses. They can be quickly installed, and the compartment size is large enough to allow adequate nesting space behind.

Materials

Bottom (3)—board, 1 by 3 by 12 in.
Sides (3)—plywood, ¼ in., 13 by 5 in.
Flathead screws (3), #8,1 in. long
Sixpenny galvanized nails (6)

Tools

Square
Ruler
Plane
Countersink
Sixpenny nail

Pencil
Saw
Drill, with ³⁄₁₆-in. bit
Hammer
Screwdriver

Instructions

A. 1. Check the width of the 1 by 3. Plane it down to 2½ in. if needed. You won't have far to go. Saw it into 4-in. lengths, squared at the ends.

2. Saw the plywood into three 4-in. lengths and plane the sawed edges lightly.

A.

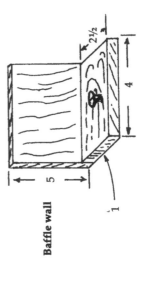

Baffle wall

Instructions

A. 1. Mark the center of the galvanized metal by drawing a line connecting the corners.

2. Tie a pencil to a piece of string. Hold your thumb over the end of the string at the center of the metal, and draw a circle that fits the size of the material, as shown. This circle should be 24 in. in diameter. In the center of the circle, draw a smaller, concentric circle about 1 in. less than the diameter of the tree. Then draw another concentric circle with a radius that is 2 in. greater than that of the tree.

3. With the tin snips, begin cutting along the outside line of the large circle. Bend the edge under, ¼ in. all around.

4. Cut from the outside edge to the center. Then cut out the small circle. Make narrow, V-shaped notches about every 1 in. around the perimeter of the small, inside circle. For the time being, cut these notches so they are ½ in. wide and 1 in. deep.

B. 1. Bend the 1-in. pieces upright to form a flange. Open the center cut and try to slip the material around the tree to check the fit. If it is too tight, make the notches a bit deeper and bend the flange pieces up so they are higher. Continue making adjustments until the metal can be overlapped several inches at the outside perimeter, forming a shallow cone when you put it around the tree. Cut off the excess to leave an overlap of 1½ in.

2. Put the metal around the tree so the cone is at least 6 ft. off the ground. Overlap the edges, forming the shape you want, then use a C clamp at the perimeter to hold the cone in position. Drive a few nails part way in to tack the flanges to the tree temporarily.

3. Drill 4 small holes, evenly centered in the overlap and from the outside perimeter of the cone to the tree. Drive in the sheet metal screws to hold.

4. Make final adjustments at the flanges to make the cone parallel to the ground, then drive in fourpenny nails to hold the cone to the tree.

B.

Placement of baffles (top view)

3. Drill a ³⁄₁₆-in. hole, centered in the face of each 1-in. block, and countersink the opening to match the head of the screw.

4. Start 2 nails along one 4-in. edge of a plywood piece. Match this, flush to the edge of a 4-in. block, and nail them together. Do the same with the others.

B. 1. One by one set each block in position on the floor near the entrance and slip a sixpenny nail into the center hole, hammering the nail into the floor about ¼ in.

2. Remove the nail, then drive a screw into each hole until the head is flush with the block. Make it snug, but not too tight. It is easier to remove at nest-cleaning time after the season. Note that by using a short-handled screwdriver, baffles can be installed with the door removed even if the roof is nailed on.

Baffle Wall for Bluebird House

Baffle walls make it harder for hawks, owls, raccoons, and cats to reach inside the box to grab nestlings. If the interior floor space is five by five inches, the baffle might be installed experimentally. With the house already built and the entrance centered as shown in the simple birdhouse design, you will need to do a little fitting.

One caution, however. As they get older, young birds crowd the entrance awaiting food brought by the parents. Without a guard beneath, a smart predator such as a cat could climb up, sit on top of the birdhouse, and hook out the youngsters one by one since escape

to the rear is blocked by others crowding the baffle platform. But this can happen even without a baffle wall. So, watch it closely and be sure to install a predator baffle on the post or pole beneath the house.

Materials

Block—wood, 1 by 3 by 5 in.
Wall—door skin (plywood), ¹⁄₈ in., 3½ by 3½ in.
Wire nails (2), #18, ¾ in. long
Flathead screws (2), #8, 1 in. long

Baffle Wall for Bluebird House

A.

Wall

Block

B.

Door

Setback 2 in.
Opening 1½ in.

Note: Dimensions are in inches

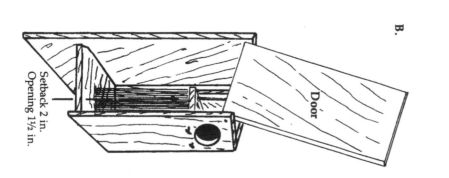

Tools

Square
Saw
Hammer
Drill, with 3/16-in. bit
Sixpenny nail

Pencil
Plane
Triangle
Countersink
Screwdriver

Instructions

A. 1. Assemble a few units in your shop to install in the field later. Start by squaring the ends of the 1 by 3-in. board, and with the nail saw, make a 5-in. long, 2 in. wide block. Square the door skin at 3½ in. by 3½ in. Plane off the splinters.

2. Start two nails 3/8 in. from the edge of the door skin. Fit it to the block, flush with the bottom and the right end. Nail them together.

B. 1. For installation in the field you will need the drill and 3/16-in. bit, a pencil, a small triangle, screws, hammer, screwdriver, and a sixpenny nail.

2. Open the side door. Hold the baffle in place, its opening nearest the door, and the top of the block ½ in. below the bottom of the entrance. Mark the spot on the edge of the front wall and extend the lines inside with the triangle.

C. 1. Run a center line across the front. Drill two holes equally spaced along this line and countersink to match the head of the screw.

2. Set the block in place. Press the nail through the front to mark locations of the holes. Lay the block down and start the nail into each mark about 3/16 in. Twist the nail to open the hole.

3. Replace the block. Hold it and start the screws. Drive them in until the block is snug.

Bluebird House Entry Hole Extender

An entry hole extender is another device that has been tested and offers some protection. When placed directly over the entrance hole, the block doubles the wall's thickness, making it difficult for predators to reach down into the nest area. The combined thickness, however, must be less than two inches. Otherwise, the bluebirds might not enter either.

Tested in the eastern part of the United States, the entry extender has met with some success. However, some anecdotal evidence exists that western bluebirds are hesitant about entering a birdhouse equipped with an extended entry.

Materials

Cedar boards, or exterior plywood, ½ in., 4 by 4 in.
Cedar boards, or exterior plywood, 5/8 in., 4 by 4 in.
Sixpenny galvanized nails (4)
Flathead screws (2), 1½ in. long

Tools

Square
Saw
Plane
Drill, with 3/16-in. bit
Sixteenpenny nail
Brace, with expansion bit set at 1½ in.

Pencil
Hammer
Countersink
Screwdriver

Baffle Block for Bluebird House: Top View

Instructions

A. 1. Square the two 4 by 4-in. pieces of plywood. Match the ⅝-in. piece on top. Place a nail near each corner and nail them together. Clinch the nails on the other side.

2. Plane the edges of the blocks to match.

3. Center a line vertically down the face of the ⅝-in. side. Place a cross mark 1¾ in. down from the top. Drill a 1½-in. hole through both pieces, centered on the cross mark.

4. Now, drill a ³⁄₁₆-in. hole halfway up the center line between the top and the upper edge of the entrance. Drill another on the center line below, halfway between the bottom and the lower edge of the entrance. Countersink the openings to match the heads of the screws. Be sure the screws slip into the holes easily.

B. 1. Place the block on the birdhouse so that the 2 entrances match. Press the sixteen-penny nail through each hole for the screws so the locations will be marked.

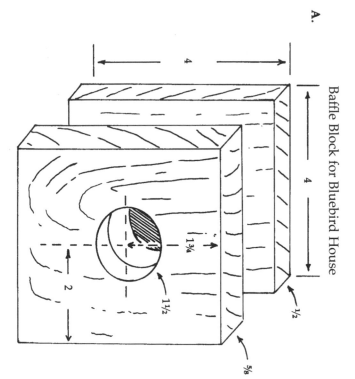

A. Baffle Block for Bluebird House

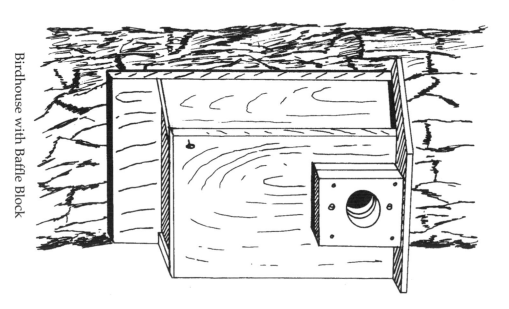

B. Birdhouse with Baffle Block

2. Remove the block. Drive the sixteen-penny nail into the marks ⅛ in. to make holes.

3. Set the block in position and drive the screws until the block is snug.

Bleach Bottle House

According to some reports, a house made out of a plastic bleach bottle seems to ward off house sparrows, but not the more desirable species. As an experimental birdhouse, it may prove to be a good way to use discarded plastic containers where a large number of accommodations are needed, such as on a bluebird trail. (In some areas bluebirds seem attracted to this type of house.)

Remember, though, to clean out the bottle thoroughly and to screw the cap on tight. To ward off the heat from the sun, the outside must have two coats of silver paint. (It dries quickly and won't bother the birds.) Vents should be cut (small holes in the sides and bottom) to promote air circulation and drainage of water.

There is one drawback. Bottles aren't easily cleaned of nest material—you will have to recycle them and start fresh each season.

Materials

Plastic bleach bottle, 1-gallon capacity
Silver paint, lacquer base or other quick-drying material
Roundhead screw, ⅜ in. long
Roundhead screw, 1½ in. long
Sixpenny galvanized nails (2)
Wood, 1 by 4 by 15 in.

Tools

Compass
Pencil
Ruler
Knife, very sharp
Drill, with assorted small bits
Screwdriver, with a screw clip
Paintbrush

Instructions

1. With a compass, make a 1½-in. circle 2 to 3 in. up from the bottom for swallows, 6 in. up for bluebirds. Use a sharp knife to cut inside the line. Then trim out a little at a time.

2. Using the ⅜-in. bit, drill 6 holes around the bottom for drainage.

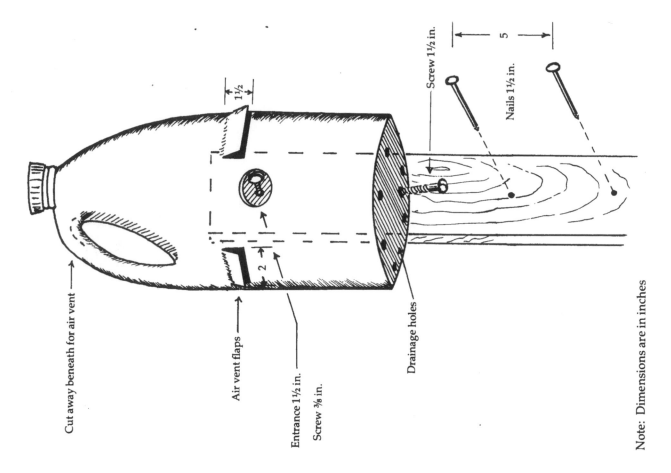

Cut away beneath for air vent

1½

Air vent flaps

Entrance 1½ in.
Screw ⅜ in.

Drainage holes

6

Screw 1½ in.

Nails 1½ in.

5

2

Note: Dimensions are in inches

3. Cut flaps halfway up the side, one on each side of the entrance, about a quarter of the way around. Make them 2 in. wide and 1½ in. tall. To ensure air circulation, bend them so they stick out ½ to ¾ in. If they do not, run a very thin stick, ½ in. wide and about 4 in. long under the flap. Tape the ends of the stick to the side of the bottle. It will help to hold the flap outward until it takes a set.

4. Underneath the top of the hollow handle, cut away a portion 1½ in. long and ½ in. wide.

5. Lay the bottle, entrance up, on the 1 by 4-in. wood, so that the bottom of the bottle extends 7 in. down from the top of the board. Mark it. Reach through the entrance with a long, narrow screwdriver, an ice pick, or even a sharp stick, and press to mark the plastic in back so it can be seen from the outside.

6. Mark the bottom, centered in line with the top. Drill through the bottom at an angle to catch both it and the side, allowing the 1½-in. screw to protrude about ⅜ in. when inserted. Turn the bottle over and drill a small hole in back where you marked it. Replace the bottle on the board and mark these spots. Remove and start a sixpenny nail in the marks.

7. Slide the clip down to the end of the screwdriver, snap the screw in place, reach through the entrance, and pin the back of the bottle to the board. (If you don't have a clip, chew gum. It's messy, but it will hold the screw long enough to get it started.)

8. Drive the 1½-in. screw into the bottom until the bottle is snug.

9. Apply two heavy coats of silver paint to the bottle. A lacquer base coat dries quickly, but give it an extra half hour just to be sure.

10. Use two sixpenny galvanized nails, spaced 5 in. apart, to mount the bottle to a tree or post. If the bark on the tree is thick, use longer nails—tenpenny or more. Don't forget the predator baffle below the house.

Suggestions

Some places are relatively free of predators, prowlers, and competitors. In other areas, they cause a constant battle. Here are some things you can try if you are beset by problems.

1. Domestic cats can be deadly to backyard birds. Most of their captures involve sick, injured, or young birds—but not always. If neighborhood cats insist on prowling your yard, let them know they are not welcome by squirting them with a hose. Eventually they will learn to scat the moment you appear. If it is your cat that's the problem, scaring it won't help. Some people believe in using a bell on the cat's collar. I've tried half a dozen—none would tinkle in time to warn the birds. Ultimately it's safest—for your cat and the birds—to keep your cat indoors. But since one cat or another will probably get into your birdhouse area, always have the houses and feeders mounted high (athletic cats can jump six feet up), and protect them with metal predator baffles.

2. If you live where raccoons, opossums, or squirrels may appear, be sure to protect your birdhouses with predator baffles. Make certain the houses are not close to structures or tree limbs that could permit an animal to cross over and gain access. Using a baffle wall is an added precaution.

3. Snakes, in most cases, will be deterred by a tightly fitted cone-type guard, or by the swinging stovepipe baffle shown earlier in this chapter. Don't depend solely on galvanized pipe as a snake-proof mount for your birdhouse. Snakes have been known to climb these, so grease the pipe with axle grease or petroleum jelly to prevent any problems.

4. Jays are known to devour eggs or young nestlings. A general precaution is never to put a perch on a birdhouse.

5. If house sparrows and starlings seem to be beating out their small competitors at your feeder, take the steps cited earlier in this chapter to control these non-native pests. Another method is to reduce your feeding of mixed seed, cracked corn, suet and peanuts. Instead, rely on black-oil sunflower seed. Sparrows

can't crack them and starlings ignore them. Most other feeder birds will be pleased at this food.

6. House wrens will peck holes in the eggs of other birds, and will even destroy the nesting attempts of bluebirds, chickadees, titmice, and martins. If house wrens are in your area, set up half a dozen small bird boxes so the wrens can stuff the entrances with twigs. Place your bluebird and martin housing out in the middle of your lawn or meadow, far from woods and hedgerows. This will effectively separate the house wrens from the other cavity-nesting species.

7. Many landlords have tried different sizes and shapes of entrances in order to discourage house sparrows from nesting in various houses. One variation is a slot that is 1 inch high and several inches wide. When used in combination with a smaller-sized nestbox (less roomy inside) the additional light the slot allows in seems to make the nestbox less inviting to house sparrows. Some landlords reduce the inside living space of their boxes by placing triangular-shaped pieces of wood in the inside upper back corner of their nestboxes. House sparrows dislike this because it makes it hard to create the canopy of grass stems they prefer in their nest building. These adaptations do not seem to bother other species. All this just goes to prove you shouldn't be afraid to experiment!

8. Elliptical entrances on nest boxes are gaining favor. The reason for the switch to an elliptically shaped entrance, is because house sparrows are able to wiggle through a narrow slot entrance, if there are irregularities left by the saw. As little as $\frac{1}{16}$ in. variance in the slot size, top and bottom, will allow them to slip through. The new elliptical shape helps to eliminate this, but it must be exactly $\frac{7}{8}$ in. at its widest point. Even so, on rare occasions, a sparrow may still get inside.

9. It may surprise you to realize that you, too, can be a competitor. Poisons in the food chain have caused untold amounts of damage to birdlife. Take it easy with the herbicides and pesticides on the lawn and garden. Certain weed killer mixtures can create havoc with night crawlers. Robins are then out of luck. Having birds frequent your yard can often eliminate many bug problems. Try to avoid using chemicals or at least use them as little as possible. It's better for your guests.

10. Starlings, bold and brassy, will often start nest building in a box you've reserved for purple martins, flickers, kestrels, or owls. Sometimes they'll even occupy a flicker box, driving out the occupants. Toss out the pale blue-green starling eggs and replace them with marbles. Chances are they'll disappear. So will the marbles. If more eggs are laid, give them the marble treatment again. It usually works, but don't expect to find your marbles. The starlings have taken them somewhere else, and no, we don't know why.

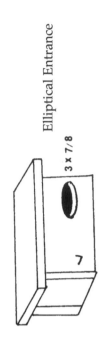

Elliptical Entrance

3 x 7/8

7

Feeders & Other Projects

By establishing a well-stocked feeder, you can have birds around throughout most of the year. This lends a bit of excitement, especially during the spring and fall migrations when new arrivals drop by while you frantically race through the bird book to establish identification. The feeder also provides you with the advantage of determining which species are the hole nesters so that you will know what sort of birdhouses to build and put up for the nesting season.

Multi-purpose Hopper Feeder

This feeding station has a number of advantages. The seed tray is independent of the housing, so you can easily lift it out, fill it or clean it, then quickly lock it back into place. That's really a blessing in nasty weather. Moreover, the tray slides in and out on cleats,

A downy woodpecker (far left) and a male rose-breasted grosbeak visit a hopper feeder.

which elevate it above the spill board, helping to keep the seeds dry during a rain. Being offset under the housing also keeps seed away from prevailing weather. At the end of the housing is a seed cake container, which holds the seed cakes under spring tension. This prevents an enterprising jay from carrying off a chunk.

Materials

Cedar boards or exterior plywood, ⅝ in., 36 by 31½ in.; or T 1-11 siding scraps:

Housing section:

Bottom—12 by 11 in.
Ends (2)—each 13½ by 8 in.
Cleats (2)—each 8 by 1 in.
Roof, left side—17 by 9⅝ in.
Roof, right side—17 by 9 in.

Seed tray section:

Bottom—10¼ by 8 in.
Cleats (2)—each ⅜ by ⅝ in.
Sides (2)—each 9¾ by 2 in.
Sides:(2)—each 10¼ by 2 in.
Ends (2)—each 7 by 4 in.
Top—11½ by 4 in.

Wood, 1 by 4 in., 2½ ft. long, ¾ in. thick
Fourpenny galvanized box nails
Flathead screws (2), 2 in. long, ³⁄₁₆ in. in diameter
Caulking compound
Hardware cloth, ½-in. mesh, 7 by 4½ in.
Small eye screws (4)
Coil springs (2),18-gauge wire, 1 in. long, ⅜ in. in diameter
Glass, 2 pieces, each 6 by 9¼ in.
Wire nails (2),1 in. long
Wooden wedges (2)—8 in. long, 1 in. wide, ⅝ in. thick
Mounting block—wood, 2 by 4 by 6 in.
Bolts (2) ¼ in. in diameter and 3½ in. long for 2 by 4-in. post; or ¼ in. in diameter and 5½ in. long for 4 by 4-in. post
Washers and nuts (2 pairs)
Post, 2 by 4 in. or 4 by 4 in., 8 ft. long (2 ft. set in concrete) or galvanized metal pole, using a pipe-flange for mounting
Prepared sand-mix concrete, 1 sack

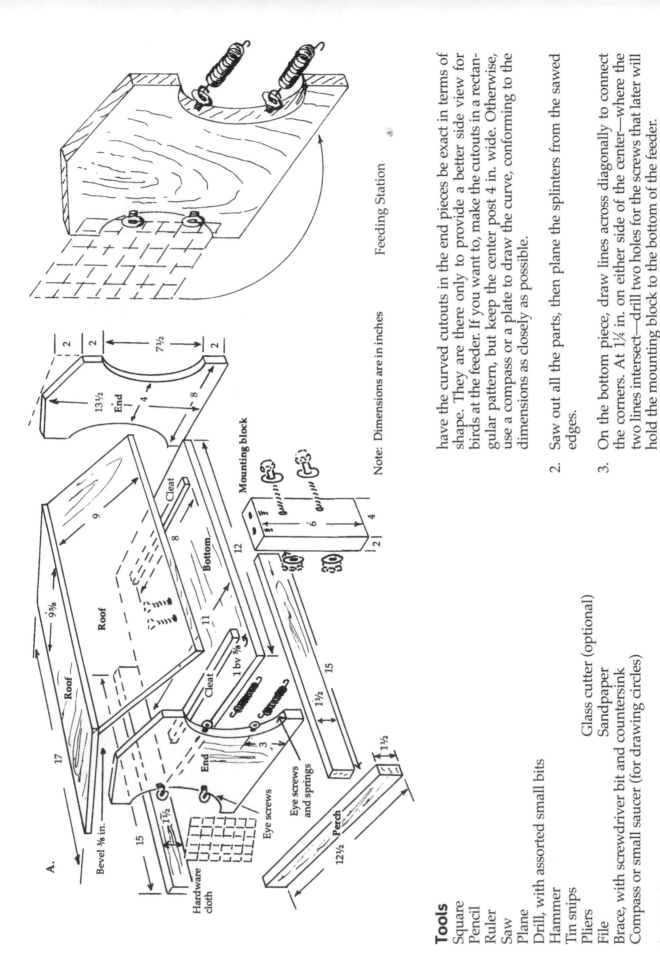

Feeding Station

Note: Dimensions are in inches

End 13½

2 2 7½ 2

4 8

Mounting block

Roof 9

9⅝ 17

Roof

Bevel ⅜ in.

15 1½

Hardware cloth

Eye screws

Eye screws and springs

End 3

Cleat 1 bv ⅝

Bottom

Cleat 8

11 12

15 1½

Perch 12½

1½

4 6 2

Tools

Square
Pencil
Ruler
Saw
Plane
Drill, with assorted small bits
Hammer
Tin snips
Pliers
File
Brace, with screwdriver bit and countersink
Compass or small saucer (for drawing circles)

Glass cutter (optional)
Sandpaper

Instructions

A. 1. Start with the main housing, shown in this drawing. Lay out the parts according to the dimensions shown. It is not critical to have the curved cutouts in the end pieces be exact in terms of shape. They are there only to provide a better side view for birds at the feeder. If you want to, make the cutouts in a rectangular pattern, but keep the center post 4 in. wide. Otherwise, use a compass or a plate to draw the curve, conforming to the dimensions as closely as possible.

2. Saw out all the parts, then plane the splinters from the sawed edges.

3. On the bottom piece, draw lines across diagonally to connect the corners. At 1¼ in. on either side of the center—where the two lines intersect—drill two holes for the screws that later will hold the mounting block to the bottom of the feeder.

B. 1. Nail on the cleats, placing them flush with the ends of the bottom piece and an equal distance from each side, as shown.

The Original Birdhouse Book

Clinch the nails beneath the bottom piece.

2. Nail the end pieces on, flush with the bottom and centered. For extra stability, put two nails through each end piece into the cleats.

3. Now for the mounting block. Drill two ¼-in. holes, equally spaced, in the side of the block. Center the block beneath the bottom of the feeder, then drill two holes through the top of the block (using the holes drilled in Step A 3 as guides), then countersink the openings and drive in the screws, using the brace (or a drill) with a screwdriver bit. It's easier.

B.

C. 1. Decide on which end you want the perch and suet feeder. Rip the 1 by 4-in. wood into two pieces, each of them 1¾ in. wide. Cut two 15-in. pieces and nail them on each side of the bottom panel, flush with the interior surface of the bottom piece and extending 3 in. beyond the suet-feeder end of the bottom. Nail the 12½-in. crosspiece to the ends of the two other perch pieces. (This makes a rather sturdy perch, but there is less danger of splitting the wood.)

2. Now for the roof. Bevel ⅜ in. off the top edge of the 9-in. roof section. Mark it for equal overhang at each end of the feeder. Tack two nails near the top, into the end sections. Lay a board along the other top edge of each end piece (where the other roof section will sit) to check that the beveled edge of the first roof section is flush with the board. Put two more nails into the end pieces, lower down, just enough to hold.

3. Lay the 9⅝-in. roof section in place to check for fit. Bevel it back ⅜ in. from the top edge, as shown. Then start two nails so they will go into the top part of the end pieces, but don't nail them in just yet.

4. Run a strip of caulking compound along the beveled edge of the first roof section you nailed on. Tack the other section in place. Check the alignment. Put in two more nails lower down, into the end pieces, and another two nails along the seam. Drive them all in.

C.

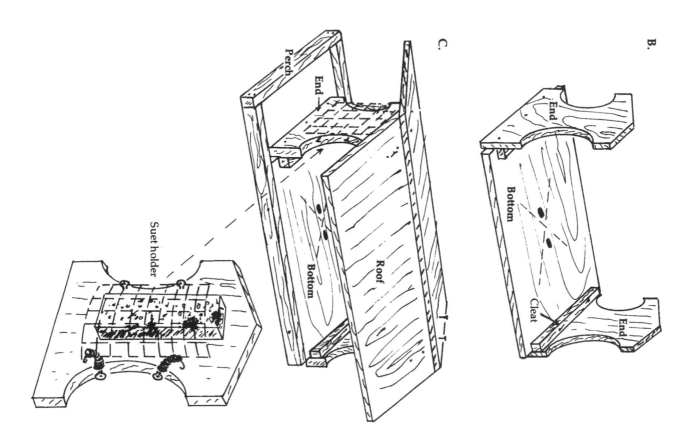

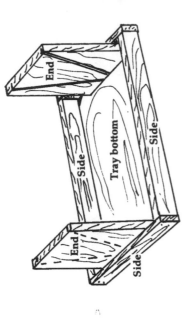

E.

5. For the suet holder, cut a piece of hardware cloth, 7 by 4½ in. Keep it flat.

6. Open two eye screws. Screw them into the end piece—¼ in. from the left edge, and 6 in. apart, the bottom screw 3 in. from the bottom. Use pliers to close them around the edge of the hardware cloth, forming a hinge. Put two more eye screws into the right edge of the end piece so they are 6 in. apart and the bottom one is 3 in. from the bottom edge.

7. Fasten two short springs, hooked through the eye screws. Use your pliers to close the hooks. As the suet cake becomes smaller, it can be held under tension by stretching the springs and sliding a loop over the edge of the hardware cloth.

D. 1. Now you can start on the tray section. Saw out all parts and trim the edges with a plane. Be sure to cut the corners back ⅓ in. on the bottom piece. This will allow drainage for the feeder and will help prevent soggy seed.

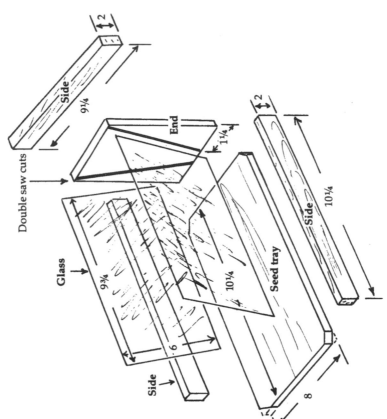

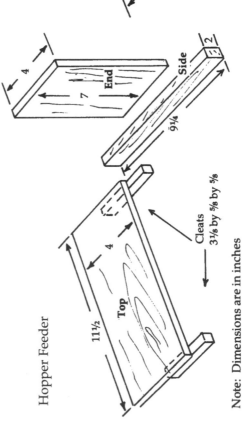

Hopper Feeder

Note: Dimensions are in inches

E. 1. On each side piece, draw a horizontal line ⅜ in. from the bottom edge. This will indicate the amount of side-drop below the bottom.

2. Nail the sides to the bottom piece, checking that they are flush with the ends of the bottom piece and matching the side-drop.

3. For the hopper, make double saw cuts into the flat side of the end sections, angled inward from the corners so they are 1¼ in. from each when they reach the bottom. These cuts should be at least ¼ in. deep. You may need to use a knife or run the edge of a thin file in each groove to clean it out.

F. 1. Fit the glass into the grooves to be sure they are deep enough. This can be done by fitting the glass piece in the slots and standing the end pieces upright in the tray. Smooth the slots with a file or sandpaper.

2. Nail the hopper end pieces, centered, inside the tray. The height of the glass can be adjusted by placing a short block ⅝ in. thick or less, under the ends. Tack them in place with a 1-in. wire nail.

3. For the top section, mark positions and nail the cleats just ⅝ in. inside the ends and an equal distance from each side. You want it to be fairly snug. (The top is necessary to prevent adventuresome birds from climbing into the hopper.)

4. Use two wooden wedges between the hopper tray and the end pieces of the housing section to hold the tray in place. The wedges should be 8 in. long, 1 in. wide, and ⅝ in. thick at 1 end, tapering to ⅜ in. at the other. You can adjust the position of the hopper under the roof, wedging it away from inclement weather when necessary.

5. Hold the feeder on top of the post, which has been set in concrete and is at least 6 ft. above the ground, and mark the post through the holes in the block. Drill ¼-in. holes and bolt the unit in place. Be sure it is equipped with a cat guard beneath (see "Predators, Pests, and Competitors" chapter).

F.

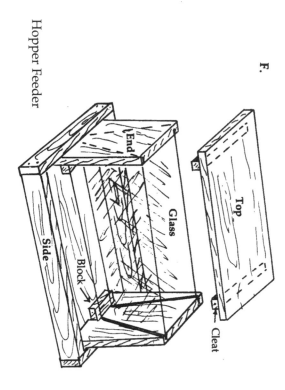

Hopper Feeder

Suet Feeder for Chickadees

With your main feeding station established and birds visiting regularly, you may want to add a few refinements. House sparrows, for example, will probably push chickadees away from the suet holder, so give the chickadees their own. But there are always the starlings, too. You can take care of the sparrow problem by building a suet holder that swings freely—sparrows don't like that. But it won't stop the starlings. The bolder ones have no qualms about swinging away as they gorge themselves. A special chickadee feeder, built only for birds with very tiny toes, will solve the starling problem, also.

Materials
Hardware cloth, ½-in. mesh; 2 pieces, each 4 in. by 6 to 8 in.
Coat hanger wire, ¼-in. diameter loops for hinges
Coil springs (2),18-gauge wire, 1 in. long, ⅜ in. in diameter
Coat hanger, straightened
Small plastic jar
Stick

A.

Hardware cloth

Tension springs

Hinges—looped wire

Suet Feeder

B.

Chickadee Seed Feeder

Perch extends ⅛ in. →

Tools

Tin snips
Tape

Pliers
Knife

Instructions

A. 1. To make your Chickadee Suet Holder, take two flat pieces of hardware cloth and put them together. Using coat hanger wire, loosely connect the edges on one side with loops (¼ in. in diameter) to form a hinge.

2. Fasten two springs to the opposite edge. When you put a suet cake between the 2 pieces of hardware cloth, simply stretch a loop of the coil over to the other edge to hold the suet cake under tension. Adjust the tension as the cake shrinks.

3. Straighten a piece of coat hanger wire until it can hook over a tree limb or under the eaves, in front of your window. Then make a smaller hook at the other end, from which you can hang the hardware cloth holder.

B. 1. To make your Chickadee Feeder, first fill a small plastic jar with sunflower seeds.

2. Tape a stick across the bottom, extending no more than ⅛ in. past the edge—just enough for chickadee toes.

3. Cut a ⅜-in. triangular hole about ¾ in. above the perch. You could make the hole round, depending on the size of the sunflower seeds. You may discover that chickadees can cling to the hole itself, not using the perch at all.

Suggestions—Feeders

In general, there are a number of things you can do to enhance the success of your feeders.

1. Any time of year is good for starting a bird feeder. Early fall is best because the birds become accustomed to it in time for the winter. Summer is least effective because then the birds' diets are predominately insects. The protein is needed for egg laying and raising the young.

2. Keep your feeder stocked well into the spring. Natural food crops may not yet be ready. If you must close down, do it gradually, in midsummer. Start it up again in the fall. You'll be surprised at some of the migrating species that stop by.

3. Birds, being highly mobile creatures, do not rely entirely on our feeders for survival. However, studies have shown that during extreme winter weather survival rates for birds with access to feeding stations are somewhat better than for birds with no feeder access. So if you must stop feeding in winter, do it gradually.

4. Wild bird and nature stores, feed stores, hardware stores, lawn and garden stores, and large supermarkets are most apt to carry commercial mixes of wild bird seed for your area.

5. Feeding birds bread is a waste of time. They need fat for extra warmth in the winter. Save all the grease you can—bacon grease, melted beef fat, everything. Mix your own seed cakes. Melt the stuff, then pour it into a cut-down milk carton or small loaf pan lined with foil. Mix in bird seed, peanut butter, raisins—whatever makes you feel creative. Cool it and store it in the refrigerator.

6. Grit is essential for birds. It is used in the bird's crop to grind food. Easily picked up year-round, it becomes a problem for the birds to find grit in heavy snow or ice. During such times, add a fine, washed sand, or eggshell bits to your feeding mixture—about a teaspoon per quart of feed is enough.

7. There are numerous kinds of plants you can grow that will supply food for the birds when they need it most. Elderberries, for example, are eaten by more than 100 different species. Check with your local bird club, garden club, native plants greenhouse, or government agency to figure out the best plants for attracting birds to your yard.

8. As a substitute for homegrown fruits and berries, you can stock your feeder with raisins, bits of apple, dried fruits, unsalted peanuts, and peanut butter. It might surprise you to see the additional species that join in.

9. Try to put your feeder within 20 to 30 feet of shrubs or trees. As with birdbaths, this gives the birds an escape route and a place to perch while awaiting turns at the feeder. Tree limbs overhead seem to give them a sense of security from danger above.

10. Birds prefer sheltered places. Most yards have enough concentration of shrubbery to provide this. In winter, place your feeding stations in a location away from prevailing weather.

11. Starlings sometimes will take over the feeders in droves. You may have to move the suet cake from the area where you have the feeder. Find an alternate location on the ground. Then dump old bread, potato peelings, anything you can think of. Starlings have a keen appreciation of garbage. Meanwhile, use only sunflower seeds at the feeder. This will make it less attractive, both to starlings and house sparrows. Chickadees, finches, grosbeaks, and others will continue flocking to your feeder. After a few days to a week, try sneaking in a suet cake.

12. If you must take a winter vacation, make arrangements with a neighbor to stop by and fill the feeder. As you bask in the sun, it will comfort you to know that most of your backyard birds are able to get food at your feeders if bad weather hits.

Roost Box

Having solved the feeder problems, for the most part, you should give consideration to a roostbox that will give the birds protection against severe winter temperatures at night. This is particularly true if you live in the Midwest or East where some winters become downright inhospitable. As many as a dozen bluebirds, for instance, have been recorded using a roost box, tucking themselves in at night, away from the bitter winds.

Materials

Hardware cloth, 1½-in. mesh, 5 by 19 in.
Perches—wooden dowels, ½ in. in diameter
Staples, #5, wire brad

Tools

Tin snips

3. Drill a series of ½-in. holes for the wooden-dowel perches, being sure to stagger the holes to prevent the birds above from soiling those beneath. Put the dowels into the wall so they extend about 4 in.

4. Complete the construction steps for the flicker box, then hang the roost box on an open tree trunk or post in the same manner as described.

Suggestions

As spring approaches, there is one more thing you might offer the birds—nest material. Making it available in safe places, off the ground, will minimize the hazards of their gathering it on the ground. A method for providing swallows with nest material already has been mentioned—distributing white feathers down the center of an open lawn. That's because swallows prefer snatching the material in mid-flight. Other species, however, search among the shrubs for nest material. Make it safer.

1. Establish a temporary post with one or two cross arms, 6 feet above ground. It needn't be a heavy timber. A 2 by 2-inch post will work, with ½-inch wooden dowels pegged through, near the top.

2. Across the dowels, lay human or animal hair clippings, wool, feathers, and short bits of yarn or string, less than 3 inches in length. Many a bird has hanged itself on a piece of string a foot long.

3. Overlay your offerings with a narrow strip of ½-inch-mesh hardware cloth. Stretch a rubber band or piece of tape across it every 12 to 18 inches. It's surprising how quickly the birds will strip away the material during nest-building season.

Roost Box

Hardware cloth

Perches (wooden dowels)

Instructions

1. Take another look at the flicker box in the chapter about woodpeckers. With some modification, it makes an excellent roost box. As you lay out the flicker box pieces, make the following adjustments: drill the entrance near the bottom, 1 or 2 in. above the floor, and make it smaller, 1½ in. in diameter. Otherwise, you may find the box filled with starlings, a true waste of your talents. Because vent space in winter is unnecessary, cut the sides ¼ in. longer than that shown in the flicker box drawing—20 in. at the back, sloping to 19 in. at the front.

2. Making necessary adjustments for the roost box, follow assembly instructions for the flicker box up to the point at which you are ready to install the side door (Step 11). Then staple a piece of hardware cloth down the interior of the back panel, floor to ceiling. This will accommodate hairy woodpeckers and downies, who roost upright, clinging to the wire.

Water for Birds

A shallow container full of fresh water that you replenish daily will do as much for attracting birds as your feeder will. Generally, birds are fearful of water that is deep at the edge. That is why birdbaths are shallow, seldom more than three inches deep at the center and sloping gradually upward toward the circumference. This gives larger birds such as robins plenty of water in which to splash around. At the same time the tinier chaps, when it is their turn, can feel safe as they disport themselves in the shallows.

Clean drinking water is important to birds, even though we may think they prefer water for cleanliness. In any case, they will come to your birdbath frequently if it is properly designed and cared for and is in a good location.

A goldfinch and a thrasher at a birdbath with a dripper.

A Simple Birdbath

You can make an excellent birdbath very quickly, using an inverted lid from a garbage can. Either set the lid on the ground and surround it with rocks, or build the following birdbath.

Materials

Galvanized metal garbage can lid
Concrete pipe with flared end, 42 in. long, 8 in. in diameter
Coat hanger wire, straightened, 36 in. long
Brick or heavy rock

Instructions

1. Place the concrete pipe, flared end down, in a suitable location.

2. Wire a brick or heavy rock and hook it on the handle of the lid.

3. Set the lid on top of the concrete stand, letting the brick or rock hang down inside the pipe. This holds the lid in place, but you can easily lift it to empty the water and clean the bath.

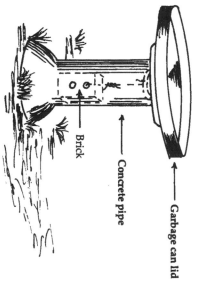

Simple Birdbath

Garbage can lid

Concrete pipe

Brick

4. Place a layer of pea gravel in the bottom of the bath to give bathing birds a less-slippery foothold.

Poured Concrete Birdbath

You will get a lot of personal satisfaction if birds splash around in a bath you have built yourself. Besides that, this bath, complete with a see-through stand, has several advantages. Light in weight, it is easily moved for mowing, and because the stand is made of hardware cloth, sunlight can get through to make the grass grow underneath the bath. With the proper circumference, the stand also is sturdy enough to hold the concrete bath securely. Built low to the ground, it gives the bathing bird an excellent visual range, with only a limited blind zone that can hide creeping predators such as cats.

It may take time for the birds to discover this new facility. Be patient. Once they do, you'll have new chores—supplying water and cleaning the bath—regularly.

Materials
Galvanized hardware cloth, 2 pieces: ½-in. mesh, 30 in. wide, 54 in. long; ¼-in. mesh, 30-in. square
Wire, 18 gauge, stove pipe, 6 ft.
Metal garbage can lid (to use temporarily as a form)
Cardboard (or chipboard), 22 by 6 in.
Large plastic garbage bag, 36 by 36 in.
Rocks, ½ in. in diameter
Prepared sand-mix concrete, 1 sack
The following materials are optional:
Faucet with a side fitting
Plastic tubing, ½ in. in diameter
Elbow, ½ in. in diameter
Necked-down fitting,¼ to ½ in. in diameter
Pet cock, to fit ¼-in. copper tubing
Copper tubing, 30 in. long, ¼ in. in diameter
Sheet plastic, 4 mil, 60 by 30 in.
Insulation or 1 daily newspaper
Light bulb, 60 or 100 watts
Outdoor electrical cord
Stake, 2 by 4 by 12 in.
Tenpenny box nails (3)

Tools
Pliers
Blocks of 2 by 4-in. wood
Masking tape, ¾ in. wide
Heavy gloves
Chalk
Galvanized pail or large pan
Small, cement trowel
Plywood, 24 by 24 in.
Tin snips
String, 18 in. long
Garden trowel
Screwdriver

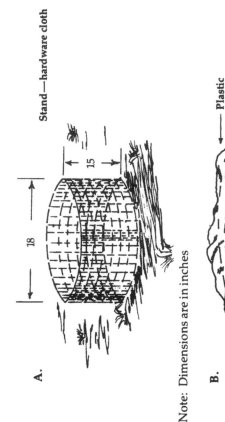

A.

Poured Concrete Birdbath

Stand—hardware cloth

15

18

Plastic

Garbage can lid

Blocks

B.

Note: Dimensions are in inches

Hardware cloth

The Original Birdhouse Book

Instructions

A. 1. To make the stand, take the ½-in. mesh hardware cloth and fold it along its length to form a strip 15-in. high. (This doubling will increase its strength and rigidity.)

2. Start gently bending the strip into a circle by making small bends in the screen as you press it around a post or the edge of the workbench. When the circle is formed, overlap the ends to achieve a diameter of 16 to 18 in. Wire the ends in place to hold the circular shape. It will now fit the standard garbage can lid. Place it on the lawn, the cut wire edges down.

B. 1. Now for the concrete basin. You will use the lid from your garbage can as a form.

2. Check all along the edge of the lid, straightening anything that is bent inward or outward. Invert the lid on 2 by 4-in. blocks to keep it steady.

3. Cut a length of cardboard, 2 in. wide. Depending on the circumference of the lid, you may need to cut several strips—the fewer the better. Set them on edge to form a collar, vertically, inside the rim of the lid. Join them end to end rather than overlapping them. Tape from the outside, over the seams, and down to the bottom of the lid. Tape a few more pieces inside against the base of the collar to hold it tight against the bottom of the rim.

4. Line the inside of the lid with plastic (doubled, if you use a plastic garbage bag). Be sure the plastic is large enough so that it drapes over the collar after you have pressed it down to mold against the lid. Line the bottom with rocks, about 1 in. apart, to hold down the plastic. (It also will allow you to use less concrete later on.) With masking tape, fasten the loose ends beneath the lid to keep them from flopping around, but do it gently without pulling, to avoid distorting the configuration inside.

5. Put on your gloves, get out the tin snips, and start on the hardware cloth. Make a cut into the center, then at the center, cut out a 1-in. hole.

6. Cut back the corners 5 in. to form an octagon, then start trimming around the outside, a little at a time, to form a circle. If you are nervous about getting a proper circle or about cutting off too much, use a piece of chalk tied to a cord. With your thumb, hold 1 end of the string in the center and swing the chalk in an arc above the screen until you find the proper radius. Then, make a series of dash marks as a cutting guide for your circle.

7. Overlap the center about 1½ in. at the outside edge, forming a shallow cone. Test the proper depth by carefully placing it on the lid. The outer edge of the cone should extend an inch or so beyond the collar, and the cone's center should be about 1½ in. above the center of the lid. When you have adjusted the overlap to achieve the correct depth, wire the cone together at the perimeter and at several spots toward the center.

8. Every 2 in. along the perimeter of the cone, cut in 2 in. toward the center. Do this entirely around the outside edge. Then lay the cone over the lid to see that the cuts end ¼ to ½ in. inside the collar. If not, make them a bit deeper.

9. Now, bend all the segments on the outside edge into a vertical position. Test the result by gently placing the cone inside the lid to see if there is a ¼- to ½-in. space between the cardboard collar and the upturned circumference of the cone. The 2-in. cuts will overlap slightly. Wire them together.

10. With pliers, begin to curl ½ in. of the vertical edge inward and down, to form an inverted J. Start with the overlapped, wired sections, then work in between, bending a little at a time until it is curled evenly all the way around. This curl is merely a kind of tuck, and it does not need to reach all the way to the bottom. Its purpose is to give a little strength and to avoid bits of wire sticking through the concrete when the birdbath is finished. Place the cone, centered in the lid and resting on the rocks.

C. 1. Drag out the sack of concrete. About half a sack should do the job—slightly less if you are efficient. Use a galvanized pail or large pan, and a garden trowel for mixing. Pour in a small amount—perhaps 1 qt.—of water. Add scoops of the dry mix until the container is about half full. You will need to add more water, sparingly, during this process.

2. Keep mixing with the garden trowel, digging the dry mix away from the sides and bottom where it tends to cling. Continue to work, heaping toward the center. Mix to a fairly dry consistency. Lifted toward the center, it should remain in chunks, but still be moist enough so that it will puddle flat, forming moisture at the surface when a trowel is jiggled over the top. So give it the old jiggle test!

3. If the mixture gets away from you and becomes soupy, don't panic. Sprinkle in a trowel of dry concrete mix and work it, adding small amounts, until you achieve the desired consistency.

4. Scrape the concrete into the lid and immediately start making another mix. Distribute each batch evenly over the surface of the lid, right up to the curled edge of the hardware cloth. Heap plenty around the perimeter so you can use it for shaping later.

5. Begin to puddle the concrete through the mesh by jiggling it with the trowel. Do this vigorously, working from the center, out toward the perimeter. Scrape excess concrete up and over the inverted J along the outer edge of the cone to support the slight ridge from the inside. This ridge need not stand up vertically. It is just a slight upturn. Make certain that none of the hardware cloth sticks above the concrete.

6. With a small cement trowel, start working from the center in long, smooth sweeps right up to the ridge. With light touches, shape and smooth the edge along the top and outside.

7. When it is finished to your satisfaction, take some blocks that will sit on the ground and reach slightly higher than the top of the basin. Place them alongside the basin, then cover them with a 2-ft. square of plywood—for protection and perhaps to avoid tiny initials appearing in your completed masterpiece.

8. For a few days after the concrete has set, sprinkle the basin lightly with a fine water mist. This slows the curing process and may help to avoid cracks, especially in hot weather. Let it cure for a week.

9. Depending on the amount of concrete used, this unit will weigh around 30 to 40 pounds. Separating it may appear to be a chore at first—you may think you'll always have a concrete garbage can lid. Keep a stout heart. It will lift out. First, turn it over. Grasp the rim with your fingers and give it a good shaking. Be careful not to drop it and crack the concrete. If you are worried about such a possibility, do this over the lawn.

10. Next, use a screwdriver to bend back the cardboard collar all the way around. Use pliers to lift out pieces of the collar. It may tear, but don't worry. Keep pulling out as much as possible.

Poured Concrete Birdbath

Hardware cloth
Plastic
Garbage can lid

c.

Eventually you will have enough clearance to slip out the concrete easily. If not, pry a bit with a screwdriver. Try working from the opposite side in case the edge of the lid is still bent slightly inward.

D. 1. Place your new creation on the low, hardware-cloth stand in the location you have chosen. To get things level, you may have to adjust the stand. Sometimes, sliding the concrete basin around on top of the stand helps.

Add a dripper

Water dripping into a birdbath enhances its attractiveness. You don't need a gushing fountain—just a drop every 2 or 3 seconds, making little rings on the surface. Here's one way to accomplish this.

E. 1. Attach an additional faucet, with a side fitting to your outside faucet.

2. Attach a length of ½-in. plastic tubing to the side fitting, and run it in a ditch through the lawn to the birdbath. (Cover the ditch, of course, once the tubing is laid.)

3. Put an elbow and a necked-down fitting at the end of the plastic tubing. Then add a pet cock and small copper tube to it. Stake it if you wish, and gently curve the copper tube over the birdbath. Adjust the pet cock, allowing the water to drip very slowly.

Add a heater

During winter freezes, birds seem to survive very well. As a rule, they don't bother to bathe. But a cold snap is often dry and drinking water can be important. To keep the bath ice free, you can use an electric water heater such as that found in a feed store for poultry raisers. In a pinch, you can use a light bulb.

F. 1. Wrap the see-through stand with black plastic. Use insulation, too, if you have any. Or you can lay out the city newspaper on a 30 by 54-in. piece of plastic, fold it into a 15-in. strip, and tie it around the outside of the see-through stand.

2. Place a 60-watt bulb in the socket of a heavy outdoor cord, and stake it in the center of the stand beneath the basin. Use 3 nails, in line up the stake. Weave the cord so that the bulb stands upright. Plug the cord into an outside socket. Use a 100-watt bulb if the cold snap is severe, switching off the light if daytime temperatures rise above freezing.

Suggestions

Your birdbath brings up a list of new considerations—the birds' safety, the bath's attraction for them, and its care.

1. Safety for the birds is an important factor, and you can do something to help out. Remember that birds need an escape zone. Try to keep the birdbath in the open, 20 to 30 feet from

D.

E.

Necked-down fitting

Elbow

Plastic pipe

Copper tubing

sides should be only about two inches high. Fill the box with very fine, dry dirt or sand and let the birds have at it. In dry weather, they seem to be more attracted if the dust box is placed in the sun where the dust can become warm.

5. To keep down the algae, clean the bath regularly, remembering never to use chemicals. It will take you only a moment to pour out the water, scrub the basin with a wire brush, and add fresh water.

6. It's possible that your birdbath will crack under the pressure of ice formation, especially if the inside edge turns up sharply, giving the ice a foothold against which to exert pressure. The shallow cone bath is less vulnerable to damage. If you are worried about your bath cracking, you can reduce the chances by placing a stick of wood in the water during cold snaps.

7. Don't throw away your birdbath if it does crack—not after all the trouble it took to build it. Simply buy a small package of high-strength cement used for mending concrete. Follow the directions, work it into the crack, and let it dry thoroughly.

F.

Light bulb and socket

Stake

Plastic folded over newspapers

Light cord

Nails

convenient cover. Brush or trees are a safe zone for them, as well as a place to perch while waiting their turns or drying off. At the same time, be careful not to place the bath *too* close to brush or trees—predators can lurk there.

2. Also, try to put the bath where it will be in shade most of the time. Birds seem to appreciate cool water, especially in summer.

3. Don't be afraid to have more than one kind of birdbath. The low, see-through stand will take care of most birds, but some will not go near unless the bath is on the ground. Try another kind to appeal to them.

4. Some bird species prefer dust baths. It's not a bad idea to have a dust box nearby, but not so close that it gets splashed with water from the bath. Place a small box—12 to 16 inches square—in the ground in a spot frequented by the birds. The

Tips for Bluebird Landlords

An incubating female eastern bluebird is fed by the male.

If any creatures in the United States need help, it's bluebirds. **Eastern bluebird** numbers, though better today, had at one time decreased by as much as 90 percent. Along the Pacific slope, the population of **western bluebirds** also declined, though not so drastically. Even mountain bluebirds have had a tough time surviving in the face of loss of habitat and competition for nesting cavities—the two main reasons for overall bluebird population declines. To conclude a book about birds without mentioning the bluebirds' plight would be inexcusable. If you have come this far, perhaps you will be one who accepts the challenge of helping these wonderful birds.

Natives of the North American continent, bluebirds are found in every state except Hawaii and every Canadian province except Newfoundland. The **mountain bluebird** is still fairly common, and can be found at medium to high elevations in the mountainous

West. The male mountain bluebird is bluish overall, distinguishing it from the eastern bluebird, which has reddish underparts, or the western bluebird, which has reddish underparts as well as some reddish coloring on the back.

All three bluebird species are about six inches long, and subsist almost entirely on a diet of insects. In winter, when insects are scarce, the bluebirds' diet shifts to fruits and berries. Although bluebirds are more active and more noticeable in the spring, they are not necessarily a warm weather bird, often lingering well into winter as long as the wild berries last.

Favoring open fields, bluebirds have a strong sense of territory and will battle another bluebird in their food zone. They traditionally nest in abandoned woodpecker holes, where they lay four to six pale blue eggs. In some cases the first brood dies, due to the harshness of early spring and the lack of insects. Fortunately bluebirds raise two, and sometimes three, broods.

The decline of the eastern bluebird has been going on for more than 60 years, though the population trend has now been reversed. Some blame this decline on agricultural pesticides. Others cite the loss of habitat (because of suburban sprawl) and the lack of wooden fence posts. Some say it is nest site competition from starlings and house sparrows that have taken every available nest cavity away from bluebirds.

Whatever the reason, bluebirds still need help—desperately. Concerned citizens in the East Coast and the Midwest have rallied to establish trails of sometimes hundreds of boxes in the countryside. Across Canada, such trails have been linked together in a chain 2,000 miles long with 7,000 nest boxes. Results are encouraging. Bluebird populations of all three species are now stable and growing slightly thanks to these conservation efforts.

Before you rush to the workshop and begin flinging together dozens of bluebird boxes, take a look at the situation. Are bluebirds occasionally seen in your area? Do you know anyone with an established bluebird trail?

Bluebird trails are really a group effort—and chances are there's a county, state, or provincial bluebird group already operating in your area. Check with your local bird club, Audubon Society chapter, or the North American Bluebird Society (contact information at the end of this chapter) to see if such a project is under way in your area. Join in! You'll learn more in less time than if you go it alone. It's a team effort, requiring careful site selection, property owner contact, transportation, accurate record keeping, map reading and making, evaluation of results, and planning for the future.

The basic design for a bluebird box is similar to that described for the first birdhouse shown in this book. It is simple to build and dozens of parts can be cut out for mass assembly.

Suggestions

Whether you're on your own or with a group, here are a few things to watch for when establishing your bluebird trail.

1. If you are interested in starting a trail of bluebird nest boxes beyond your own property, you will need to get permission from the landowners to enter and locate the boxes. Explain the project, pointing out the need for frequent inspections and the fact that these chores might be performed by someone *other* than yourself. Make a detailed map. List the landowner's name and phone number so you can call ahead if you need to make arrangements.

2. It may be necessary to establish a line of 15 to 20 boxes to enhance your chances of attracting bluebirds. Once you have breeding birds established in your boxes, you will have more birds nesting each year as family groups return.

3. Search for locations such as pasturelands or open fields, preferably interspersed with a few old hardwoods. Avoid cultivated fields—of wheat, for example. It grows tall and dense, and the bluebirds cannot see their insect food, the bugs.

4. Bluebird boxes placed in farmyards, in suburban settings, or other inappropriate bluebird habitat will attract house sparrows, house wrens, and starlings. Bluebirds may also be forced to seek out new territories, and you might have to move the boxes. One idea is to move the unused boxes to areas where you find ample bluebirds.

5. Inspect the boxes frequently—at least once a week. This is necessary in order to keep records of weather conditions, arrival dates, number of eggs, incubation periods, condition of the young, predator damage, nest abandonment, and so on. Analysis of this information will aid in improving the trail.

6. When inspecting a box, do not stomp heavily up to it, jerk open the door, and thrust your face in. Young birds, not quite ready to fly, may be startled into leaving the nest. Then you've lost the ball game— returning them is more difficult than putting toothpaste back into the tube. Approach slowly, with caution. Scratch on the side of the box to alert the female to leave. Open the door just a crack. Nearly grown young birds will tend to crowd into a corner. Let it go at that. Make a mental note of your findings (number of nestlings, age, sex, appearance, nest condition), close the door quietly, and steal away. Younger birds are less apt to be startled. Your notes should tell you which boxes contain those old enough to be jittery.

7. Cease your nest box visits when the young bluebirds reach 12 days of age. Before 12 days, the nestlings are too young and undeveloped to fly. After 12 days they are very spookable. Begin counting the days from the date that the eggs hatch.

8. Although bluebirds have been successfully raised in boxes as low as two to three feet off the ground, five to six feet is better. You will want them low enough for easy inspection. For this reason the side door is more convenient than the top opening, unless you like to carry a stepladder. And *aim* the box, facing it away from prevailing winds and weather. In most parts of North America, facing the entry hole to the east is best. A snag or tree 50 to 100 feet in front of the entrance will be readily used by adults and fledglings.

9. Mount your bluebird boxes on 8-foot galvanized metal pipe, ¾-in. diameter. Sink 2 feet of the pipe into the ground. Mount a predator baffle below the box, and mount the house 5 or 6 feet off the ground. Unless you are sure there are no nest box predators in your area, avoid the temptation to wire the boxes to the sides of metal fence posts or mount them on top of wooden posts. Especially avoid doing this in cattle country. Cows like to scratch and often knock off the boxes. To circumvent this problem, use an extension board so that the box is above the cow's reach. Do not put bluebird houses up at all in pastures where horses graze. A horse scratches higher than a human can stretch conveniently.

10. Because these birds depend on a staked-out territory to feed the young, place western and mountain bluebird boxes 400 to 600 feet apart, eastern bluebird boxes 300 feet apart.

11. Avoid locations near human habitation, such as farmhouses and barns. That's house sparrow country. House sparrows will take over an established bluebird nest box by pecking holes in the eggs, and killing the incubating female bluebird. Also avoid large thickets or brush piles likely to harbor house wrens. They might take a fancy to the bluebird box and nest there. The house wren, too, punctures eggs, or it may simply plug the hole with sticks, rendering the box useless to the bluebird.

12. In areas with *no* nest box predators, tree trunks make excellent locations so long as the box is not hidden by low limbs. Be sure the box is vertical or tipped forward slightly, not backward. Rain gets into the hole.

13. Boxes should be in place and ready when the birds arrive. Check local authorities to determine arrival dates in your vicinity. Generally, late winter is a good time.

14. Although you can clean out the boxes after the nesting season, usually in fall, there are some good reasons for doing it in spring, just before the nesting season. If bees or wasps have taken over, you can get them out before the bluebirds come and are repelled from the boxes. In some areas summer blowflies can also be a problem. Occasionally they lay eggs in the boxes. The grubs that later hatch are harmful to young birds. However, a certain species of tiny wasp also lays its eggs in the boxes and its hatchlings destroy the grubs. Spring cleanout gives the wasp a chance, in areas where this is a problem.

15. Remove the old nest and thoroughly clean out the box before the new nesting season begins.

16. To discourage mites and blowflies, clean out dirty nests and scrub the box interior out with a light bleach-water solution. *Do not use rotenone or any other chemical inside the box.* Nestling bluebirds have very thin skin and any toxic chemical they come into contact with can harm them. A good time to remove the nest-lings from a badly soiled or mite-infested nest is when the young are about a week old. Make a replacement nest out of soft, dry grass, formed into a cup shape. Simply put the new nest in the box, and put the nestlings in the new nest. I take a grass-lined bucket along for holding the nestlings temporarily when I'm doing nest changes.

17. Check and keep records on each nest to determine its seasonal history—fledging success, number of eggs, abandoned eggs or young, types of nest material, dead birds, and other indicators.

18. Leave the boxes up in winter. This gives other birds a place to escape severe weather, especially in northern climates.

19. Be sure to use the simple method of mounting a bird box that you might want to move. Screws can be more easily removed than nails. When using a galvanized pole and strapping brackets or a pipe flange for mounting, loosening the screws permits easy box removal.

For More Information

North American Bluebird Society
The Wilderness Center
P.O. Box 244 • Wilmot, OH 44689-0244
888-235-1331 • **www.nabluebirdsociety.org**

Bird Watcher's Digest & The Backyard Bird Newsletter
PO Box 110 • Marietta, OH 45750
800-879-2473 • **www.birdwatchersdigest.com**

Purple Martin Conservation Association
Edinboro University of Pennsylvania •Edinboro, PA 16444
814-734-4420 • **www.purplemartin.org**

Cornell Laboratory of Ornithology/Birdhouse Network
159 Sapsucker Woods Road • Ithaca, NY 14850
800-843-2473 • **www.birds.cornell.edu/birdhouse**

American Bird Conservancy
PO Box 249 • The Plains, VA 20198
888-247-3624 • **www.abcbirds.org**

U.S. and Metric Measurements

Measurements in *The Original Birdhouse Book* are given in the U.S. form of measurement. Those who prefer to use the metric system will find the following conversion table useful:

inches x 25 = millimeters
inches x 2.5 = centimeters
feet x 30 = centimeters
feet x 0.3 = meters

10 millimeters (mm) = 1 centimeter (cm)
10 centimeters (cm) = 1 decimeter (dm)
10 decimeters (dm) = 1 meter (m)

Birdhouse and Shelf Dimensions

The following is a summary of important measurements for birdhouses and shelves. There may be variations. For example, tree swallows and violet-green swallows can enter a hole 1¼ inches in diameter instead of 1½ inches (so can the house sparrow). The purple martin of the West has been known to enter a hole ¾ inches in diameter, instead of 2 inches (so can the starling, according to some authorities). And, although a 4-inch entrance is common for wood duck boxes, the one described in this book calls for a 3 by 4-inch entrance, rounded on the horizontal, because it helps to discourage raccoons.

Nor is there a hard-and-fast rule for interior dimensions. These are averages. Birds often accept nest boxes larger or smaller than those listed for the species, as long as they can gain entrance. Perhaps this is due to a shortage of natural nest cavities. With wood-peckers, your chances of success may be improved if you pack the box full of wood chips.

Birdhouses

Species	Entrance Diameter	Entrance above Floor*	Depth of House	Inside of House	Height above Ground
Bewick's wren	1 in.	1 to 6 in.	6 to 8 in.	4 by 4 in.	6 to 10 ft.
House wren	1 in.	1 to 6 in.	6 to 8 in.	4 by 4 in.	6 to 10 ft.
Carolina wren	1⅛ in.	1 to 6 in.	6 to 8 in.	4 by 4 in.	6 to 10 ft.
Chickadees	1⅛ in.	6 to 8 in.	8 to 10 in.	4 by 4 in.	6 to 15 ft.
Downy woodpecker	1¼ in.	6 to 8 in.	8 to 10 in.	4 by 4 in.	6 to 20 ft.
Nuthatches	1¼ in.	6 to 8 in.	8 to 10 in.	4 by 4 in.	12 to 20 ft.
Titmice	1¼ in.	6 to 8 in.	8 to 10 in.	4 by 4 in.	6 to 15 ft.
Tree swallow	1½ in.	1 to 5 in.	6 in.	5 by 5 in.	10 to 15 ft.
Violet-green swallow	1½ in.	1 to 5 in.	6 in.	5 by 5 in.	10 to 15 ft.
Eastern and western bluebird	1½ in.	6 in.	8 in.	5 by 5 in.	5 to 10 ft.
Mountain bluebird	1⁹⁄₁₆ in.	6 in.	8 in.	5 by 5 in.	5 to 10 ft.
Hairy woodpecker	1½ in.	9 to 12 in.	12 to 15 in.	6 by 6 in.	12 to 20 ft.
Red-headed woodpecker	2 in.	9 to 12 in.	12 to 15 in.	6 by 6 in.	12 to 20 ft.
Golden-fronted woodpecker	2 in.	9 to 12 in.	12 to 15 in.	6 by 6 in.	12 to 20 ft.
Purple martin	2 in.	1 in.	6 in.	6 by 6 in., at least	15 to 20 ft.
Northern flicker	2½ in.	14 to 16 in.	16 to 18 in.	7 by 7 in.	6 to 20 ft.
Screech-owls	3 in.	9 to12 in.	12 to 15 in.	8 by 8 in.	10 to 30 ft.
Kestrel	3 in.	9 to 12 in.	12 to 15 in.	8 by 8 in.	10 to 30 ft.
Wood duck	4 in.	18 to 20 in.	24 to 26 in.	10½ by 10½ in.	10 to 25 ft.
Barn-owl	6 in.	4in.	15 to 18 in.	15 by 18 in.	12 to 18 ft.

*Entrance above floor is measured from the center of the entrance to the floor.

Shelf Nests

Species	Sides	Depth of House	Inside of House	Height above Ground
Barn swallow	1 or more sides open	6 in.	6 by 6 in.	8 to 12 ft.
Phoebes	1 or more sides open	6 in.	6 by 6 in.	8 to 12 ft.
Robin	1 or more sides open	8 in.	8 by 8 in.	6 to 15 ft.
Song sparrow	All sides open	6 in.	6 by 6 in.	1 to 3 ft.

Further Reading

The Backyard Birds Newsletter, BWD Press, P.O. Box 110, Marietta, Ohio 45750. 800-879-2473. **www.birdwatchersdigest.com**

Barker, Margaret A. and Griggs, Jack. *A Cornell Bird Library Guide: The FeederWatcher's Guide to Bird Feeding*. New York: HarperCollins Publishers, Inc., 2000.

Berger, Cynthia; Kridler, Keith and Griggs, Jack. *A Cornell Library Guide: The Bluebird Monitor's Guide*. New York: HarperCollins, 2001.

Bird Watcher's Digest, P.O. Box 110, Marietta, Ohio 45750. 800-879-2473. **www.birdwatchersdigest.com**

Bird Watchers Digest's Backyard Booklet Series, BWD Press, P.O. Box 110, Marietta, Ohio 45750. 800-879-2473.

The Backyard Booklet Series includes:
• *A Guide to Bird Homes*
• *The Backyard Bird Watcher's Answer Guide*

Dennis, John V. *A Complete Guide to Bird Feeding*. New York: Alfred A. Knopf, Inc., 1994.

Dennis, John V. *A Guide to Western Bird Feeding*. Marietta, Ohio: BWD Press, 1991.

The series includes the following titles:
• *An Identification Guide to Common Backyard Birds*
• *Enjoying Hummingbirds More*
• *Enjoying Bird Feeding More*
• *Enjoying Squirrels More (or Less!)*
• *Understanding Bats*
• *Enjoying Purple Martins More*
• *Enjoying Bluebirds More*
• *Enjoying Woodpeckers More*
• *Enjoying Butterflies More*
• *Creating Your Backyard Bird Garden*
• *Creating Your Water Garden*

Ehrlich, Paul R., Dobkin, David S., and Wheye, Darryl. *The Birder's Handbook*. New York: Simon and Schuster, Inc., 1988.

Henderson, Carrol L. *Woodworking for Wildlife: Homes for Birds and Mammals, 2nd edition*. Collingdale, Pennsylvania: DIANE Publishing Company, 1995.

Kaufman, Kenn. *Lives of North American Birds*. New York: Houghton Mifflin Company, 1996.

Thompson, III, Bill. *Bird Watching for Dummies*. New York: J. Wiley & Sons/Hungry Minds/IDG Books Worldwide, Inc., 1997.

Wild Bird Guides. Mechanicsburg, Pennsylvania: Stackpole Books, 2000.

The series includes the following titles: Black-capped Chickadee, Northern Cardinal, Tufted Titmouse, Red-tailed Hawk, American Goldfinch, Downy Woodpecker, Ruby-throated Hummingbird, Eastern Bluebird

Zickefoose, Julie. *Natural Gardening for Birds: Simple Ways to Create a Bird Haven*. Emmaus, Pennsylvania: Rodale, Inc., 2001.

Index

Notes:

Notes: